DETERMINED
MEN WHO STAND STRONG WITH UNYIELDING RESOLVE

JOE WELLS, M.MIN.

DETERMINED: MEN WHO STAND STRONG WITH UNYIELDING RESOLVE
Copyright © 2024 by Kaio Publications
http://www.kaiopublications.org

All rights reserved. No part of this publication may be reproduced, stored in a retrieval system, or transmitted in any form by any means, electronic, mechanical, photocopy, recording, or otherwise, without the prior permission of the author, except as provided for by USA copyright law.

First printing 2024
Printed in the United States of America

Scripture quotations taken from the New American Standard Bible® (NASB), Copyright © 1960, 1962, 1963, 1968, 1971, 1972, 1973, 1975, 1977, 1995 by The Lockman Foundation
Used by permission. www.Lockman.org.

ISBN: 978-1-952955-49-5

Grammar edited by Tonja McRady
Cover and interior design by Kristin Arbuckle

DETERMINED

RISE ABOVE THE NOISE, THE COMPROMISE, & THE PASSIVITY TO TAKE AN UNCOMPROMISING STAND FOR GOD AND HIS WAYS.

DETERMINED
TABLE OF CONTENTS

INTRODUCTION — 6

CHAPTER 1: DETERMINED TO INCREASE — 9

CHAPTER 2: DETERMINED TO PAY ATTENTION — 27

CHAPTER 3: DETERMINED TO DO RIGHT — 45

CHAPTER 4: DETERMINED BE RIGHT — 67

CHAPTER 5: DETERMINED TO STAND — 87

INTRODUCTION

In every generation, God has called men to possess an unwavering faith and be steadfast in pursuing righteousness. This is a calling, not restricted to a selected few, but is meant to go forth to every man who desires to follow Christ. The world around us is filled with distractions, temptations, and challenges that threaten to pull us away from our true purpose. Yet God calls us to live with determination, to pursue Him without yielding. This book, ***Determined: Men Who Stand Strong With Unyielding Resolve***, is an invitation to men everywhere to rise above the noise, the compromise, and the passivity to take an uncompromising stand for God and His ways.

At the very heart of this call into determination is a pursuit of spiritual growth. As men, we have been called to lead in our families, congregations, and communities. We have been called to grow in the knowledge of God, letting His Word shape our hearts and turn us into men of depth, character, and unshakeable commitment to Christ. This is not a passive journey. It takes intentionality, effort, and the will to press forward even when the road is hard.

While this book speaks to your personal walk with God, it also speaks to a greater responsibility. As men, we are called to be the spiritual leaders of our homes. Whether you are a husband, father, or mentor, your determination to follow Christ will impact not only your own life but the lives of those around you as well.

Your family needs you to be strong in the Lord. They need to see the faith at work in your life. This can't just be evident for an hour or two on Sundays. They need to see this in your everyday life. As you prioritize growing spiritually, honor God's Word, and do right, you model an example for your children. You are the anchor that holds your family fast to the true Shepherd. By standing firm in your commitment to Christ, you're building a spiritual heritage that will carry on for generations.

This book is designed to inspire, encourage, and equip you for a determined life. But it also comes with a warning: The life of faith is not for the faint of heart. It requires toughness, stamina, and resolve as the storms rage and the waves crash against you.

The stakes are high. Your walk with God is at risk, and your family's spiritual well-being hangs in the balance. You don't have to walk this journey alone. God is with you, and He's given His Word to equip you and the Church to support you.

So, let's begin the journey. Let's commit to being men of determination. As we do, let's watch how God will use our lives to bring glory to His name, strengthen our families, and impact the world for Christ.

Will you be determined?

CHAPTER 1
DETERMINED TO INCREASE

"We all have dreams. But in order to make dreams come into reality, it takes an awful lot of determination, dedication, self-discipline, and effort."[1]

- Jesse Owens -

Special Section: Synonyms of *determined*:

Resolute—**fully committed to achieving a goal**

Being resolute is a powerful trait that can help us achieve our goals and overcome obstacles. Resolute people have a clear sense of purpose and are determined to achieve their objectives, no matter what. They have a clear vision of their goals and are committed to reaching them. They have a strong will. Setbacks or failures do not easily deter resolute people. They have a strong sense of self-discipline and are willing to put in the effort needed to achieve their goals. They are also willing to sacrifice and endure discomfort if it means getting closer to their objective.

The quality of being resolute means having a positive mindset. Resolute people are optimistic and believe success is possible and probable. They do not let negative thoughts or self-doubt hold them back. Instead, they focus on their strengths and capabilities and use their failures as opportunities to learn and grow. They are adaptable and willing to adjust when necessary.

Being resolute is not just about being determined to achieve your goals. It's also about being committed to your values and beliefs and staying true to them even in adversity. Resolute people have a strong sense of integrity and are guided by their principles, which gives them a sense of integrity and are guided by their principles, which gives them a sense of purpose and direction. They are honestly aware of their strengths and weaknesses and use this knowledge to make informed decisions regarding areas they need to improve, being determined to reach their goals.

Perseverance and patience are crucial. Resolute people understand that success does not come overnight and that achieving their goals may require hard work and sacrifice. They are willing to put in the effort and stay committed to their objectives, even when slow progress or setbacks occur.

HISTORICAL EXAMPLE

Thomas Edison, one of the most prominent inventors of the 19th century, was well known for his relentless determination to succeed. Born in 1847 in Milan, Ohio, Edison was one of seven children. Samuel and Nancy Edison were his parents, and his father worked as a shingle maker and carpenter. Edison had very little formal education and was mainly homeschooled by his mother. Despite his lack of formal education, Edison was a bright child and showed an early interest in science and technology.

Edison's first job was as a train newsboy, selling passengers candy and newspapers. However, he soon became interested in telegraphy and began working as a telegraph operator at 15. During this time, Edison first began experimenting with electrical devices, and he soon became known for his ingenuity and creativity in electronics.

In 1869, Edison moved to New York City, establishing his first laboratory and working on his many inventions. Over the next few years, Edison would develop several groundbreaking technologies, including the phonograph and the incandescent light bulb. However, despite his many successes, Edison faced numerous setbacks and failures along the way.[2]

One of Edison's most famous failures was his attempt to develop a storage battery for electric cars. Despite working on the project for over a decade, Edison was ultimately unsuccessful and the battery was never brought to market. However, instead of giving up, Edison continued to work on other projects and eventually invented the alkaline storage battery, which became widely used in the 20th century.

Another of Edison's failures was his attempt to create a machine that could transcribe spoken words onto paper. Despite working on the project for years, Edison could never get the machine to work correctly and eventually abandoned the project. However, his work on the machine ultimately led to the development of the phonograph, which became one of his most successful inventions.

Perhaps one of Edison's most famous quotes is, "I have not failed. I've just found 10,000 ways that won't work."[3] This quote perfectly sums up Edison's attitude towards failure. Instead of viewing failure as a negative thing, Edison saw it as an opportunity to learn and grow. He believed every failure was simply a step towards success, and that the key to success was never giving up.

Edison's determination and perseverance are what ultimately led to his success. Despite facing numerous failures and setbacks throughout his lifetime, he refused to give up on his dreams. He constantly pushed the boundaries of what was possible and always looked for new and innovative ways to solve problems.

Edison's legacy continues to inspire people today. His inventions revolutionized the world, and his determination and perseverance serve as a reminder that anything is possible if you are willing to work hard and never give up. Edison's life is a testament to the power of determination and the importance of perseverance in achieving success.

In 2 Peter, we read of a determination far more significant than Edison's—that of the apostle Peter. With the writing of this letter being dated between 64–68 A.D., we are left with the conclusion that Peter's time on this earth is short (2 Pet. 1:14). In instances such as these, we often see people leaving their last impressions, their last "words of wisdom" some might say. In Peter's situation, it's no different. He cares deeply for the recipients of this letter, referring to them as "*beloved*" no less than five times in chapter 3 (vv. 1, 8, 14, 15, 17). He is determined for them to remain established in the truth. It compels him, with one of the final strokes of his pen, to stir or "*awaken*" them to decide, be firmly determined, to increase in their spiritual walk as God demands of those whom He calls through the Gospel (2 Thess. 2:14; 2 Pet. 1:3, 10, 13).

DISCUSSION

As our attention turns to the text of 2 Peter 1:1-11, we learn five crucial components that must be present if we are determined to grow spiritually. In 2 Peter, we see this determination to increase is pivotal in combating atrocities of the false teachers, their "*destructive heresies*" (2 Pet. 2:1) and their immoral lifestyles engulfed in "*sensuality*" (2 Pet. 2:2). In reflecting on our own culture today which is inundated with greed, saturated with rampant teachings that go against Scripture, and the sexualization of even the most innocent aspects of society, absolute determination to grow is unapologetically necessary. In other words, if the Holy Spirit inspired the apostle Peter to instruct these Christians to set their purpose and determination to grow spiritually firmly, you and I must do the same today if we are going to hold fast to our walk with God and lead our families to do the same in our cultural context.

What five crucial components must be present to be a determined person who desires to grow spiritually?

1) We must sincerely appreciate what God has already done for us.

Fundamental to every aspect of growth in your life is a complete appreciation for where you are in life and where you are going. When a person sets out to better himself occupationally, he must understand not just how far he's come from the early days in his job but why and how he arrived at the place he is. This period of reflection allows him to learn from his past and appreciate where he currently is. It also will serve as a significant motivating factor to continue to press on to that next level.

The same holds true when applied to several other areas of our lives. Weight loss, healthy lifestyles, creating new habits, developing a deeper level of Bible study, improving our personal relationships, and a host of other aspects of each of our lives are all impacted by reflecting in the mirror and appreciating how we arrived we are and what we've learned along the way. Only after taking inventory do we find the motivation to change or improve in areas in which we are underperforming.

In 2 Peter, this need to remember and appreciate reverberates throughout the first chapter. Peter draws these Christians back to the work that God has already accomplished through the righteousness of Jesus Christ (v. 1). This precious faith they possess, like that of the apostle Peter himself, is not cheap, nor is it to be weak.

Through the tremendous demonstration of sinlessness while walking this earth (2 Cor. 5:21), Jesus continually entrusted Himself to the Father as He endured extensive persecution and hatred (1 Pet. 2:23). With an unswerving determination to live according to the divine standard of the Father, Jesus accomplished precisely what He was sent to this earth to do: *"seek and save that which was lost"* (Luke 19:10). It's because of the love of God, demonstrated in and through the crucifixion of His only begotten Son Jesus, that you and I, just like the Christians to whom Peter is writing in our text, bask in the grace and peace that God abundantly supplies (John 3:16; 2 Pet. 1:2). God has richly provided everything we need that pertains to life and godliness, both here on this earth and in eternity (2 Pet. 1:3).

Therefore, as we reflect on our escape from the corruption of our previous life and the fact God has allowed humanity to know Him through the written Word, Peter says we have the *"precious and magnificent promises of God"* in which we place our complete trust (v. 4). We have the firm assurance from God who is not like man and who cannot lie (Heb. 6:18). Because of who He is and what He has done, we don't have to die in our sins (Rom. 6:23).

It's fascinating that Peter begins with this message, emphasizing the nature of God, which expresses God's nurturing of humanity through Jesus Christ. He shows that God has done far more for you than you will ever be able to do for Him, and He wants the recipients of this letter to appreciate this fact unequivocally and deeply. By beginning with this point, Peter draws a very important message to the pinnacle: If you are going to be the person who is determined to increase spiritually, you must first appreciate what God has done for you in Jesus Christ. Another way to express this would be that if spiritual growth is not occurring in our lives, it's not because it's too complicated and unrealistic. We do not fully and sincerely appreciate what God has done for us.

Is that challenging? It's meant to be. That's what Scripture does in the heart of the person seriously seeking God and allowing His Word to convict him. Do you want to know if you are genuinely determined to increase? The answer begins with whether the fire of your appreciation for God's work in your life through Jesus has died down or worse—gone out.

2) We must be ready to apply and supply diligently.

The thought of accomplishing something personally positive is attractive to many. For example, consider the resolutions people make immediately after the New Year begins. On January 2, the workout facilities are packed, whereas just days before, the "regulars" could use any machine anytime. Now, because of all the "newbies" who have made resolutions to grow and increase their physical health, they must wait in line. Some may promise to eat healthier, run/walk every day, and some will even resolve to study their Bibles or go to worship/Bible class more regularly. While these are all excellent goals and aspirations, the question is, "Why do so many people fail at keeping their resolutions?"

In an article posted on psychologytoday.com entitled, "Why Do Resolutions So Often Fail?" author Gurnek Bains, Ph.D. noted what he believes is the number one answer to this question.

> *The answer is simple. The one constant we carry is the same old self. Too often, we confuse a change in context with a change in self.*
>
> *It's very common. Think about a time when you've looked forward to a new job, a new relationship, a big move, or even just a new wardrobe. We assume that once we get this shift in our environment or situation, this will somehow automatically trigger a transformation of our character. We can leave our insecurities behind and emerge, the myth goes, into happier, more confident, successful people.*
>
> *If only meaningful change were so easy. The truth is that as long as we take the same self into any new situation, the problems we encounter are likely to re-emerge. This is why people often encounter the same conflicts in different relationships, the same insecurities being replicated in new jobs or the same junk food items being scoffed from the fridge two days after your pledge to eat more healthily.*[5]

Did you catch that? Here's the quote, "The truth is that as long as we take the same self into any new situation, the problems we encounter are likely to re-emerge." In other words, if a resolution will stick and there is lasting change, we can't simply show up at the gym or the church building and expect that to do the trick. There must be a change inside us if there will ever be lasting change outside us.

Peter begins by drawing the Christians back to what God has done in their lives. When a person obeys the Gospel, God causes him to be born again to a living hope (1 Pet. 1:3). Paul writes to the Christians in Rome regarding this new birth that a new walk will be present because a newness of life is now a reality (Rom. 6:4).

However, in Romans 12:2, the apostle Paul emphasizes where the root of any external change occurs in our lives when he writes,

> *And do not be conformed to this world, but be transformed by the **renewing of your mind**, so that you may prove what the will of God is, that which is good and acceptable and perfect.* (emp. added)

Peter also homes in on the importance of the internal readiness of the mind when he pens,

> *Therefore, **prepare your minds** for action, keep sober in spirit, fix your hope completely on the grace to be brought to you at the revelation of Jesus Christ.* (1 Pet. 1:13; emp. added)

Again, in 2 Peter 1:15, he writes of the importance of what the mind is thinking about righteous living,

> *All I will also be diligent that at any time after my departure you will be able to call these things to **mind**.* (emp. added)

It could be said that where the mind goes, the body will follow. Therefore, if you want purity of body, purify your mind. If you want to improve your relationships, improve how you view others. If you're going to increase spiritually in your physical walk before God, you must grow in your internal determination and commitment to such an end. That's the significance of 2 Peter 1:5.

> *Now for this very reason also, **applying** all **diligence**, in your faith **supply** moral excellence, and in your moral excellence, knowledge.* (emp. added)

For now, notice the following impactful words in this verse:

- **"Applying"**—[*pareisphéro*] make every effort, do your best [6]

- **"Diligence"**—[*spoudé*] earnest commitment in discharge of an obligation [7]

- **"Supply"**—[*epichorēgéō*] to provide (at one's own expense) [8]

What do these all have in common?

They each require an internal conviction that causes an external action. If we are going give our very best effort, show up with an earnest commitment, and be willing to sacrifice whatever is necessary to provide at our own expense what is required to reach the goal, we must be unapologetically convinced in mind, heart, and our very being that the end for which we strive is right and good. If we have doubts or lack of conviction mixed into our thought process, we will fail in one of these areas, if not all. Initially, we may be like the sprinter who bursts out of the blocks when the starting gun sounds. However, like the runner who fades when the muscles get tired and the lungs begin to burn, if we are not determined to diligently apply and supply what God tells us is necessary for spiritual growth, the enemy will overtake us (2 Pet. 3:8).

God will not force you to grow. He has done His part through Jesus Christ and has made it possible for us to know Him. However, we must decide, here and now, and every day from this point forward, that we will give our total and determined commitment to God. We will pay the price, whatever that may be. Like Paul, we will *"press on toward the goal for the prize of the upward call of God in Christ Jesus"* (Phil. 3:14).

3) We must possess, not merely dabble.

In Acts 3, we read of Peter and John in Jerusalem going up to the temple at the hour of prayer. Just as they were about to enter the temple, a man described as "lame from his mother's womb" (Acts 3:2) began begging them to give him alms, that which is benevolently given to meet a need, primarily of a material nature.[9] Demanding the lame man's attention, Peter said, "I do not possess silver and gold, but what I do have I give to you: In the name of Jesus Christ the Nazarene – walk!" (v. 6).

Focus for a moment on the word *possess*. In the Greek, it means "to really be there, exist, be present, be at one's disposal."[10] Understandably, then, what Peter is telling the lame man is he has no silver and no gold. If he did have any, he could not say, "I do not possess" because that would be a lie. In other words, there is a clear and definitive distinction between possessing and not possessing something.

While this may sound like a lesson parents would teach their child trying to make the case that they didn't take their sibling's toy when they did, sometimes using the most straightforward logic and explanation helps make the most profound point. There is a big difference between possessing something and not.

Now, focus your attention on 2 Peter 1:8,

> *For if these qualities **are yours** and are increasing, they render you neither useless nor unfruitful in the true knowledge of our Lord Jesus Christ. (emp. added)*

Here, we see the same word translated as "*possess*" in Acts 3:6 included in the translated phrase "*are yours.*" The meaning is the same, only the emphasis is more clearly stated. Peter tells the Christians receiving this letter that the referenced qualities must be genuinely present in their lives. They must own them, having made a clear and firm decision that these qualities aren't merely something they dabble in throughout their lives but ones they own.

Unfortunately, many Christians will spend the entirety of their lives believing, or at least practicing, that if they attend worship and are pretty good people at home, they will be pleasing in the eyes of God. Their spiritual growth is seen as a passive exercise if they even see it as exercise. They obeyed the Gospel, show up for worship, and go about their lives.

That couldn't be further from what this text is teaching. At some point, a line of determined commitment must be drawn in the sand of our lives. There must be a "point-of-no-return" where we decide we are all in and that a plan B doesn't exist. There is no going back for the determined Christian who dares make this commitment. The ships have been burned, and the only way to move is toward the increase.

Faith is your starting point, not the end. Like a house that cannot be built except upon a solid foundation, your life must have the firm foundation of a stable and sure faith. A high level of trust in God and obedience to His Word is fundamental; however, the apostle Peter makes it very clear that if, like the Christians to whom he is writing in 2 Peter, we are going to be able to withstand the continual onslaught of those who seek to derail our faith and encourage the participation in the unrestrained corruption offered by the world by lust (1:4), then we must be determined to continually grow as a follower of Jesus Christ.

Where should we be focusing our efforts when it comes to being determined to increase? Consider what Peter writes by inspiration of the Holy Spirit in 2 Peter 1:5-7.

> *Now for this very reason also, applying all diligence, in your faith supply moral excellence, and in your moral excellence, knowledge, and in your knowledge, self-control, and in your self-control, perseverance, and in your perseverance, godliness, and in your godliness, brotherly kindness, and in your brotherly kindness, love.*

Moral Excellence	uncommon character worthy of praise, excellence of character, exceptional civic virtue
Knowledge	comprehension or intellectual grasp of something spoken of practical knowledge, discretion, prudence
Self-control	restraint of one's emotions, impulses, or desires, self-control
Perseverance	the capacity to hold out or bear up in the face of difficulty, patience, endurance, fortitude, steadfastness, perseverance
Godliness	awesome respect accorded to God, devoutness, piety, godliness
Brotherly Kindness	sense of affection for a fellow-Christian used of the love of Christians one to another, brotherly love out of a common spiritual life
Love	the quality of warm regard for and interest in another, esteem, affection, regard, love

Don't get wrapped up in the order of these virtues. Like the instruments in an orchestra, they are individually significant and can stand on their own. Like a violin soloist captivates and deeply draws the audience in, each of these qualities or Christian virtues does the same. However, imagine a cellist joining the violin soloist on the stage. As they combine their beautiful sounds and melodies, the song intensifies as it intertwines in the listener's mind. As the soft sound of the flute is added, the thundering percussionists join, and the rest of the artists play their distinct instruments in the orchestra; the collective sound of the orchestra is complete, each instrument complementing the next.

That's the concept we should have when considering this list. It's not considered a stair-step system where we master the first and then move on to the second. Instead, you and I are to possess, not dabble in, each of these qualities simultaneously as part of our being. If that's going to happen, a determined decision must be made. Just as was mentioned at the beginning of this section, there is a difference between possessing something and not possessing it. You can't sort of possess something. Either you possess it, or you do not.

So, do you possess faith, moral excellence, knowledge, self-control, perseverance, godliness, brother kindness, and love?

4) We must be increasing in each of these qualities.

In 2 Peter 1:8, the Greek word for "increasing" is πλεονάζω, "*pleonázō*," from the root πλέον, "*pleon*."[11] It's defined as "to become more and more, so as to be in abundance, be/become more or be/become great, be present in abundance, grow, increase."[12] At first, using this word may not seem like a significant key to unlocking the deeper meaning behind what Peter is writing; however, a fuller picture begins to appear when we understand this word.

Imagine sitting in an old-fashioned diner, drinking a cup of coffee, and enjoying breakfast. Your waiter comes by the table and notices that your coffee cup is about half-full, so he kindly asks if you would like more coffee. As he begins to pour the fresh, hot coffee into your cup, you notice the coffee getting very close to the top edge. You assume he will stop before it's too late; however, without hesitation, your waiter continues to overflow the coffee into the saucer below. He's not apologetic. He simply wanted to make sure you have an abundant amount of coffee.

If you were sitting at the table in the diner and something like this happened, you may not be too happy. After all, who wants to participate in the daring endeavor of lifting a full cup of hot coffee from the table to his lips? However, this is offered to illustrate the meaning behind the word "increasing" in this text. The intricate details of this word encompass the idea of overflowing or abundance. There's more than is needed, and the coffee is not limited to the edge of the cup. Instead, it overflows. The word *pleonázō* is that word. Here, Peter is saying these virtues not only must be present in your life but there is also no limit to how much they must be increasing and overflowing in your life.

In Romans 5:20, by inspiration of the Holy Spirit, the apostle Paul used this same word to emphasize how great the grace of God is when he wrote, "*The Law came in so that the transgression would **increase**; but where sin **increased**, grace abounded all the more*" (emp. added). Here, the word is used in correlation with the Law of Moses and man's inability to keep it perfectly. Thus, when the Law was made known, sin increased as man missed the mark of such. Paul answers that "*grace abounded all the more.*" The word *abounded* is impressive because it means the abounding is supercharged. No matter how much sin increase—and no limit is set by this word—grace is supercharged and can more than cover the enormous amount of sin.

Consider these other verses where we find this word.

- Mark 4:8—"*Other seeds fell into the good soil, and as they grew up and **increased**, they yielded a crop and produced thirty, sixty, and a hundredfold.*"
- Luke 2:52—"*And Jesus kept **increasing** in wisdom and stature, and in favor with God and men.*"
- John 3:30—"*He must **increase**, but I must decrease.*"

- Acts 6:7—"*The word of God kept on spreading; and the number of the disciples continued to **increase** greatly in Jerusalem, and a great many of the priests were becoming obedient to the faith.*"
- 2 Corinthians 9:10—"*Now He who supplies seed to the sower and bread for food will supply and multiply your seed for sowing and **increase** the harvest of your righteousness.*"

In each of the above, the idea being relayed using the word *pleonázō* is growth without reference to a cap or a limit. What is significant is that in all the above verses and the many more throughout the New Testament that could have been referenced here, the word *increasing* is not a neutral term. It never implies staying at the same level or reaching maximum growth without needing to grow continually.

If we are people determined to increase, there must be a mindset present where we understand we are not working toward a minimum level of increase where God will be pleased. Instead, our mindset must be set on continually growing in moral excellence, knowledge, self-control, perseverance, godliness, brotherly kindness, and love.

5) We must practice, not merely memorize.

Perhaps one of the greatest struggles for many who study God's Word is not found in memorization but in implementation. Since we were little children, many of us have been taught songs that encouraged committing to memory the books of the Bible, the 12 apostles, and the days of Creation. From the earliest years of our lives, we were taught to memorize and recite Scripture. We studied for Bible Bowls and took tests to see how much we retained. Perhaps we even gave speeches at competitions designed to help us grow our knowledge of God's Word and the presentation of Bible lessons/sermons. These are all great and should be encouraged among every child in a Christian home. However, memorizing songs, Scripture, facts, and speeches alone will never please God if the facts, Scripture, and lessons don't change that person's walk before Him.

In business, there are "Thinkers," "Doers," "Talkers," and "Watchers."

While most leadership and business websites address the necessity for each in the business environment, they also talk about the dangers that exist if there is a lack of balance and cohesion between these groups. While some in the company need to come up with a plan, effectively communicate it, and measure its success or failure, at the most basic level of the company, someone must implement the plan putting it into action. Meetings can take place all day long, and charts can be created; however, if no one is willing to work hard on the plan, the plan remains a hypothetical theory that may or may not be worthwhile.

According to one author, the difference between "Talkers" and "Doers" can be summarized in three areas: risk, focus, and execution. The "Doer" understands and accepts the risks. He isn't blind to them. He simply decides to manage them instead of allowing them to paralyze him from doing anything. "Talkers" discuss all the beautiful things they want to accomplish; however, they fear what could go wrong. Thus, they stay in meetings, dreaming of what could be. "Doers" are focused and accomplish something every day. They do not explain why they couldn't "get around" to a task like the "Talkers." Instead, "Doers" make a plan and are determined to accomplish something, even if just a tiny portion of the task every day. The "Doer" knows that all the small steps cover a significant distance when added together. Execution is about regular and steady progress daily, and the "Doer" is determined toward execution.[13]

In your spiritual walk, you must become a "Doer." It's not enough to merely study the Word of God and be able to quote a lot of verses. This statement is not meant to belittle the importance of studying the Word of God (2 Tim. 3:15). However, the Word of God was never handed down to us so that we could memorize sections and impress one another with how much we know. It was meant to be a lamp to our feet and a light to our path (Ps. 119:105). The Word of God is to be written on our hearts and souls, meaning the core of who we are (Deut. 11:18). Scripture was handed down to us to inform us and move us because of the Good News found therein.

That's why Peter, in 2 Peter 1:10, tells the Christians and us that we must be practicing—doing— these virtues he outlines. Christianity is an active lifestyle, not a passive study. With faith as my starting point, I must practice moral excellence, knowledge, self-control, perseverance, godliness, brotherly kindness, and love. Being a "Talker," "Thinker," or "Watcher" is not enough. Here, Peter says we must be "Doers."

CONCLUSION

To the average person, it could be said that Thomas Edison failed more than he succeeded. However, one thing that separated Edison from most people was his resoluteness. He was determined to continue moving forward and learning along the way. He believed the outcome was obtainable and all the sacrifices along the way were completely worth the cost. To Edison, the seeming failures only brought him closer to his desired end. He was determined to grow, learn, advance, and accomplish.

Are you determined to increase your spiritual walk? Do you have an unwavering resolve to stay committed through whatever difficulties come your way? Do you have a sincere appreciation for what God has done for you? Are you ready to diligently apply and supply everything He instructs? Do you possess these Christian virtues outlined in 2 Peter 1? Do you own them, or have you been dabbling in them occasionally? Are you increasing in each of these areas today? Are you practicing these, or are you merely talking about them?

I call these "crossroad questions" that are meant to place you at a pivotal point in determining which way you will go. That's important because if you are going to be a determined person in your walk with the Lord, you must get off the fence and make a definitive decision. John 15 clarifies that no unproductive branches will be left to hang out on the vine. You are either growing and producing or merely taking up space on the vine. Spiritually speaking, a determined man doesn't stand at the crossroads and take solitude simply in knowing how God wants them to go, all while he remains stagnant and cemented in the ground. Instead, the determined man will commitment to increasing in the direction God has outlined in Scripture.

REFLECTION

1. How is culture impacted when a man of God commits to growing spiritually?

2. How does reflecting on your escape from sinful corruption serve you as you look ahead?

3. Do you agree with this statement: "The truth is that as long as we take the same self into any new situation, the problems we encounter are likely to re-emerge?" Why do you agree/disagree?

4. What would you say if you had to explain to a child the difference between possessing or not possessing something? As you reflect on this, can you say you possess the qualities mentioned in this chapter? If not, why not?

5. What difference does it make if a person has a mindset that they are growing to a specific point compared to when they are growing and will never be done growing? What impact could each of these mindsets have on a man?

| NOTES |

CHAPTER 2
DETERMINED TO PAY ATTENTION

"An invincible determination can accomplish almost anything and in this lies the great distinction between great men and little men."[1]

- Thomas Fuller -

Special Section: Synonyms of *determined*:

Purposeful—**having a purpose; meaningful; intentional; full of determination**[2]

Being purposeful in life is one of the most important things you can do to live a meaningful and fulfilling existence. It means having a clear sense of direction and working towards goals that align with your values and beliefs. Purposeful living can help you stay motivated, focused, and happy.

Here are some tips on how to be purposeful in life.

First, take the time to reflect on your values and beliefs. What matters most to you? What do you believe in? What are your passions and interests? Once you understand what you value, you can start setting goals and making decisions aligning with those values.

Next, set realistic and achievable goals. Your goals should be specific, measurable, and time bound. For example, if your goal is to write a novel, you could set a goal to write for an hour every day and have a completed manuscript within a year. Having clear goals will help you stay on track and measure your progress along the way.

Third, take action towards your goals. Break your goals into smaller, manageable steps and take action towards them every day. Staying committed to your goals is essential, even when things get tough. Remember that setbacks and failures are a natural part of the process and can help you learn and grow.

Fourth, surround yourself with supportive people. A network of people who support and encourage you can help you stay motivated and focused on your goals. Seek like-minded individuals who share your values and interests and can offer guidance and support.

Living a purposeful life is not only beneficial to your personal growth, but it can also positively impact those around you. You inspire others when you have a clear sense of direction and work towards goals aligning with your values and beliefs. Your dedication and commitment can motivate others to pursue their goals and live purposeful lives.

HISTORICAL EXAMPLE

Colonel Harland Sanders is a man who is widely known for his famous fried chicken chain, Kentucky Fried Chicken. However, most people don't know that he was determined and faced numerous obstacles and setbacks before succeeding.

Sanders was born in 1890 in Indiana. His father died when he was only six years old, forcing him to take up various odd jobs to support his family. Despite this, he managed to finish sixth grade and went on to attend high school. However, he dropped out before graduating to work as a farmhand.

In 1917, Sanders enlisted in the U.S. Army and served during World War I. He was honorably discharged in 1919 and returned to his hometown in Indiana. He then took various jobs, including selling insurance and running a ferryboat company. However, none of these ventures were successful, and he struggled to make ends meet.

In 1930, Sanders opened a small restaurant in a gas station in Corbin, Kentucky. He started selling his famous fried chicken, which he had perfected over the years. The restaurant became popular, and he expanded his business by opening franchises. However, in 1952, disaster struck when a new interstate highway was built, bypassing Corbin and causing a significant drop in business.

Undeterred, Sanders embarked on a journey to promote his chicken recipe to other restaurants across the United States. He drove around the country in his car, sleeping in it and cooking for restaurant owners willing to try his recipe. He faced numerous rejections but was determined to succeed.

Finally, in 1955, Sanders signed a deal with a restaurant owner in Utah, who agreed to pay him a royalty for every piece of chicken sold using his recipe. This began the KFC franchise, one of the world's most successful fast-food chains. Sanders continued to work tirelessly, traveling around the world to promote his brand and ensure that the quality of his chicken was consistent across all locations. He also became known for his eccentric personality, dressing in a white suit and black string tie and sporting a goatee.

Despite his success, Sanders remained humble and committed to his values. He believed in providing high-quality food at a reasonable price and treating his employees and customers respectfully. He also donated generously to various charities and organizations.

In 1980, Sanders passed away at 90, leaving a legacy of hard work, determination, and innovation. Today, KFC has over 23,000 locations in more than 140 countries, serving millions of customers every day.

Colonel Harland Sanders is an inspiring figure who embodies the values of determination, perseverance, and hard work. Despite facing numerous setbacks and rejections, he never gave up on his dream of bringing his famous fried chicken to the world. His legacy inspires countless individuals worldwide to pursue their dreams and never give up, no matter how difficult the journey may be.

Driving in the snow and ice is not for the faint of heart. I spent my middle and high school years in western Pennsylvania learning to drive. To stay off the roads during the winter months is not an option there, so I quickly learned the value of having good tires that firmly and securely grip the road. We were taught that it wasn't a matter of if we would slide while driving but when. We approached the journey expecting it to be complicated. Therefore, we learned to read the road, anticipating the most dangerous parts. Time and time again, it was drilled into our minds what to do if you begin to slide and what the most effective maneuver would be to get your vehicle back into alignment where the tires could firmly grab the road.

This concept of having good and solid contact between the tires and the road can be applied to many different areas of life. In 2 Peter 1: 12-15, the apostle writes concerning this same principle,

> *Therefore, I will always be ready to remind you of these things, even though you already know them, and* **have been established** *in the truth which is present with you. I consider it right, as long as I am in this earthly dwelling, to stir you up by way of reminder, knowing that the laying aside of my earthly dwelling is imminent, as also our Lord Jesus Christ has made clear to me. And I will also be diligent that at any time after my departure you will be able to call these things to mind. (emp. added)*

The phrase "*have been established*" expresses this same "tire-gripping" concept. The Greek word for "established" means "to cause to be inwardly firm or committed, confirm, establish, strengthen" and is used multiple times throughout the New Testament.[3]

- Luke 22: 31-32–"*Simon, Simon, behold, Satan has demanded permission to sift you like wheat; but I have prayed for you, that your faith may not fail; and you, when once you have turned again,* **strengthen** *your brothers*" (emp. added).

- Acts 18: 23—*"And having spent some time there, he left and passed successively through the Galatian region and Phrygia, **strengthening** all the disciples"* (emp. added).
- 2 Thessalonians 3:3—*"But the Lord is faithful, and He will **strengthen** and protect you from the evil one"* (emp. added).

In each of these instances, there is a determination expressed intent on firmly fixing and setting fast those who are disciples of Jesus Christ. Just as the winter storms rage in western Pennsylvania as they did when I was growing up, some storms crash into the lives of those who seek to be set apart for the purpose of God. Those who desire to be faithful will find "slick spots" along the way, and there must be a purposeful determination to read the road. More importantly, like the tire to the road, a determined connection must be made and maintained with the Word of God.

DISCUSSION

A simple principle in following a map while driving says that whatever route you take, you will end up where it leads. It may not be the most profound statement you've ever heard; however, it is true. If you want to go to Los Angeles, you better take a road that leads west towards California. If you began going east toward New York believing you were going to Los Angeles, you would be sorely mistaken upon seeing the Statue of Liberty. However, if you pick the path that leads to Los Angeles and stick to it, you will see the beautiful Hollywood hills which you were seeking. If you desire a destination, you had better pick the path that leads you there.

In driving, this is a simple concept. However, what about the areas of philosophy and religion? Is it possible for the path to appear to take you in the right direction only to find out after following it for too long that it leads the opposite way? If you're not careful and paying attention, then "yes." In philosophy and religion, there may be just enough truth sprinkled in with complete fabrications of man that all paths may seem right to the one who is leisurely strolling along the way.

It's so sad to think about, but that's precisely what is happening today. Postmodernism, evolution, humanism, materialism, and countless other philosophies are promising answers with no power to deliver on them. Happiness and fulfillment remain elusive to those rummaging through the garbage pile of beliefs abundant in our culture today. There's just enough substance for these and the numerous religious beliefs floating about to captivate those strolling through life. To those who are not determined, all paths appear correct. However, the differences are very apparent to those determined to pay attention.

In 2 Peter 1:19, Peter writes, "*So we have the prophetic word made more sure, to which you do well to **pay attention** as to a lamp shining in a dark place, until the day dawns and the morning star arises in your hearts*" (emp. added). Interestingly, Peter stresses the responsibility these Christians possess regarding where they give their attention. He emphasizes the importance of such by using this word that, in Greek, means "*to pay close attention to something, pay attention to, give heed to, follow.*"[4] A constant state of being alert and continual care is stressed. However, why would he tell them such, and why would they determine to pay attention as he has strongly encouraged? The answers in 2 Peter 1: 12-21 are just as applicable and meaningful for us today. When we more fully understand what they were facing and how they would avoid the derailments, we will be more firmly grounded and determined to pay attention to the prophetic Word ourselves.

What does it take to be determined to pay attention to anything, especially to the prophetic Word, as Peter instructed?

1) Being convinced it is worthy of my attention.

In 1997, I was a freshman at Texas Christian University in Ft. Worth, Texas. I was considered "undeclared" in my major, which meant I was in the process of taking as many introductory liberal arts courses as possible that the school required. One of those classes was basic science in a lecture hall with over one hundred other students. It was your typical first-year level class taken by the masses because we didn't know what we wanted to do with our lives yet, but we had to mark a science class off our list.

About mid-semester, we were introduced to four guest lecturers who were all considered professionals in their specific area when it came to the subject of evolution. I had just turned 18 and was grossly unprepared for the onslaught of evolutionary teaching I received. At first glance, their material sounded pretty good. After all, they were the ones with the initials behind their names, and I was a kid trying to figure out life away from home. It became easy to be drawn into their explanations and theories, although I didn't even really understand what a theory was at the time. They taught as if their conclusions were settled and there were no rebuttals or arguments to be made against them. So, like the hundreds of other first-year students in the class, I took notes and tests, regurgitating the information I had ingested.

My confusion became bothersome because all my life, I had been taught that God created everything in the six days of Creation as outlined in Genesis chapters 1 and 2. I never questioned it, so in my first year of living on my own, I was bombarded with this new belief system that is touted as scientific fact. Fortunately, my grandparents lived in Waco, Texas, and I went to see them on the weekends. During one of those visits, my grandmother and I sat in their driveway while I told her about my class and the confusion that boiled up. I remember even asking her if it were possible that the Bible and my teachers were correct simultaneously. With great patience and confidence, my grandmother took the time to explain the Word of God to me. She reminded me that the Bible claims God made each creature after its kind and that the days of creation were literally 24-hour days. I later found out this is known grammatically by the use of the Hebrew word *"yom"* combined with a clarifier, *"there was evening and there was morning"* (Gen. 1:5, 8, 13, 19, 23, 31).[5]

I invite you into a pivotal time in my early years to illustrate the power of philosophies rooted in manufactured myths and fables. Evolution, macro-evolution, as taught in many schools throughout the world, is universally known as a theory, meaning it has never been proven and given accreditation to make it a law. In the field of science, once something has been repeatedly tested time and time again and demonstrated the same results, it is moved into the category of a law, such as the law of gravity. However, if a belief gets stuck in the theory stage, some hurdles and obstacles can't be overcome. Thus, for many, a belief that remains stagnant in that stage for an extended period should be dismissed. Instead, for this myth, this fable simply known as the theory of evolution, our society allows it to be used to sway the innocent and impressionable minds of our youngest toward a belief that God is not nonexistent, the Bible is not credible, and that humans are simply a higher form of animals and thus act as such.

"Cleverly devised tales" is Peter's phrase in 2 Peter 1:16 to describe these empty and man-made philosophies and ideologies in which some ground their trust and confidence. Like the guest lecturers in my freshman science class who crafted their conclusions based upon unfounded myths and legends passed down in writings of misguided individuals, those who devised the tales present at the time of Peter's writing did so for various reasons. As we will see in the following chapters, dishonest men introduced destructive heresies for their own gain (2:1). That's nothing new. These "false words" (2:3) are broadly cast because of the greed in the sower's heart. We've got to be more discerning than merely allowing every proposed truth to seep into our hearts and be the road our "tires" grip.

When I accept and agree with the premise that whatever road I take, I will end up at a specific destination, I will understand the road is worthy of my attention. If I am going to be a determined, purposeful person, then the route I take matters. It matters in my relationships, occupation, parenting, hobbies, and, most importantly, my relationship with God. So, should the road we take, the philosophies and religious teachings we adhere to, be worth our attention? Absolutely! However, we must be genuinely convinced of this fact.

2) Being convinced the one telling me is trustworthy.

Each of us, in both large and small ways, encounters discerning moments daily. We hear or read news reports that are processed through filters that have been set in our minds and hearts. We read books where philosophies are applied, and perhaps religious conclusions are propagated. Through these filters, we weigh what is said to determine if it is logical and routed in authenticity. We will discern whether to allow those teachings to influence and change us. That's why it's essential to be convinced of the trustworthiness of the person declaring such.

Peter was not a man without flaws. While there are books upon books written about the historical data surrounding his fishing business, his marriage, and his teachings, to test the trustworthiness of the man calling others to listen to his words and count them as truth, we must evaluate his character. It's been said before, "The only thing that walks back from the tomb with the mourners and refuses to be buried is the character of a man. What a man is survives him. It can never be buried." [6] Peter's character lives beyond his grave, whether in Rome or wherever. The man's character demands that we pay attention to his writings.

Peter had numerous wonderful qualities. He was **bold**, as demonstrated in Matthew 16:21-23 when Jesus told the disciples He was going to go to Jerusalem and *"suffer many things from the elders and chief priests and scribes, and be killed, and be raised up on the third day."* Peter, refusing to allow any such thing to happen to his friend and teacher, pulled Jesus aside and seriously began to rebuke Him. What a ridiculous reaction from Peter! However, it reveals a fundamental quality of his character. Peter was very bold.

Peter was also **decisive**. In Matthew 14, in the face of fear (v. 26), Peter cried out to Jesus and said, *"Lord, if it is You, command me to come to You on the water."* The Scriptures leave us no reason to conclude there was hesitation on Peter's part after Jesus said, *"Come"* (v. 28). Peter decisively stepped out of the boat on the stormy sea and briefly walked on the water.

He was **courageous**. On the night Jesus was betrayed, Peter was with Him in the garden. John 18:3 records the scene this way, *"Judas then, having received the Roman cohort and officers from the chief priests and the Pharisees, came there with lanterns and torches and weapons."* Having a Roman cohort present means there could have been as many as 600 soldiers with weapons of war strapped to their bodies.

These would have been battle-trained and tested men, and Peter's response was to be the first to pull his sword and strike. Jesus healed Malchus (v. 11) and told Peter to put his sword away; however, think about Peter's courage on that momentous occasion.

Peter was **insightful**. While many thoughts about Jesus circulated during his day, Peter keenly observed and listened to what Jesus did and taught. It doesn't mean he fully understood everything the Master did; however, he also knew Jesus was more than John the Baptist, Elijah, Jeremiah, or other prophets. When Jesus asks, *"But who do you say I am?"* Peter answers, *"You are the Christ, the Son of the living God"* (Matt. 16:15-16). Jesus affirms that this insight had not come from the wisdom of men. Instead, Jesus responded, *"Blessed are you, Simon Barjona, because flesh and blood did not reveal this to you, but My Father who is in heaven"* (v. 17).

While these and numerous other positive traits give a glimpse into Peter's character, they also only paint a partial picture. Peter was a man who could be **distracted with fear and doubt**, as he displayed in Matthew 14 when he took his eyes off Jesus and began to look at the stormy sea. He was filled with an **over-abundance of self-confidence** as revealed in the upper room of Matthew 26 when, upon hearing Jesus tell the disciples they will all fall away because of Him (v. 31), Peter brazenly replied, *"Even though all may fall away because of You, I will never fall away"* (v. 33). Seeing this overconfidence, Jesus replied, *"Truly I say to you that this very night, before a rooster crows, you will deny Me three times"* (v. 34). Peter vowed that he would die before ever doing such; however, we know how that ended next to a fire in the courtyard.

Along with these, Peter **struggled with hypocrisy**, especially when it came to the interactions of Jews and Gentiles. The most notable was in Antioch when Paul had to confront him to his face. Paul records details about this interaction in Galatians 2: 11-21 and states,

> *But when Cephas came to Antioch, I opposed him to his face, because he stood condemned. For prior to the coming of certain men from James, he used to eat with the Gentiles; but when they came, he began to withdraw and hold himself aloof, fearing the party of the circumcision. The rest of the Jews joined him in*

> *hypocrisy, with the result that even Barnabas was carried away by their hypocrisy.* (v. 11-13)

Perhaps the most considerable dent in the armor of his character is when he **fearfully denied Jesus** three times on the night He was betrayed (Matt. 26: 69-75). Some have pointed out that Peter displayed great courage in showing up to the courtyard in the first place. Perhaps that is true. After all, when he cut off the ear of Malchus, he would have become known among the group who took Jesus, the same group that would logically have been at the gathering that night. Even if this is a moment of courage, Peter's denial of Jesus, amplified by cursing in the third denial, was about saving his own skin. Fear overcame, doubt clouded, and self-preservation kicked in.

The true character of any man is understood, not by diving deep into each aspect and allowing that one to define him completely. Instead, a man's character is like a soldier's armor. Some portions reveal battle scars, clashes, and piercings. Perhaps there are stains of blood, sweat, and the filth of the battlefield ingrained in the seams. However, there are sections where the sword has not pierced, and the club has not dented. Some portions have withstood the filth of battle and reflect what appears to be perfection. Overall, the soldier's armor tells a complete story that can only be understood when taken as a whole.

In the same manner, the character of Peter, just like ours, is best understood in totality, and the whole picture is that Peter repented and would go on to bravely advance the cause of Christ throughout the known world of his day. He would stand with the others on the Day of Pentecost, declaring the saving message of the Gospel of Jesus Christ (Acts 2). After having been imprisoned and threatened to never speak in the name of Jesus Christ again, he, along with John, stood their ground and declared, "*Whether it is right in the sight of God to give heed to you rather than to God, you be the judge; for we cannot stop speaking about what we have seen and heard*" (Acts 4:19-20). He's the same Peter who history will record that shortly after writing the book of 2 Peter, would watch his wife crucified and would himself be crucified, possibly upside down, because he would rather die for the cause of Christ than deny him, saving his own life (see John 21:18-19).

An individual who devotes his life to advancing a message and is willing to die for such is either a lunatic or has a firm conviction rooted in what he knows. In 2 Peter 1:16, Peter makes it very clear that he is not a madman. Instead, he claims to be an "eyewitness" of the majesty of Jesus Christ. He was there on the Mount of Transfiguration and saw firsthand what occurred. The Scriptures record that Jesus was *"transfigured before them; and His face shone like the sun, and His garments became as white as light"* (Matt. 17: 2). He was an "earwitness" in that he heard with his ears when the Father said, *"This is My Beloved Son, with whom I am well-pleased; listen to Him"* (v. 5).

Apart from having a flawless character, Peter is a trustworthy witness when taken as a whole. Through a testing and tumultuous journey, his character was shaped and molded into the older man we read in 1 and 2 Peter. Even with the "warts" Peter possessed, Jesus saw an honest man who, when convicted, would decisively move to advance what was right and good, even if it meant dying for that cause. That tells me everything I need to know about the man admonishing the recipients of this letter, as well as you and me today, to pay attention.

3) Being convinced it is God's Word.

If I devote my life to a teaching that advances a belief rooted in a resurrected Messiah, I better be convinced, without any doubt, that teaching is truly from God. In 2 Peter 1:20-21, Peter writes, *"But know this first of all, that no prophecy of Scripture is a matter of one's own interpretation for no prophecy was ever made by an act of human will, but men moved by the Holy Spirit spoke from God."* Drawing a stark contrast between the *"cleverly devised tales"* (v. 16) of the false teachers of his day, Peter makes it crystal clear that the Scripture (v. 19) is very different than anything these Christians would ever hear and read. Whereas many philosophies and religious beliefs are rooted in man's interpretations and their desired conclusions, Scripture is not. Instead, Peter claims Scripture is given to us by men *"moved by the Holy Spirit"* who *"spoke from God."* Since that is the case, we should be able to see clear and credible evidence that these men weren't simply coming up with prophecy as they went along.

What would such evidence look like, and where can we turn to observe it? Consider the following reasons why you should be convinced that Scripture is unlike any *"cleverly devised tales"* made by the *"interpretations"* of man according to their *"human will."*

Fossil Record: The Bible tells us that God created all living things and that each species was created according to its kind (Gen. 1). This idea is supported by fossil records, which show that living things appear suddenly and fully formed rather than gradually evolving. Along with this, for a fossil to form, an organism that was once living had to be quickly and wholly covered with sediment so that the oxygen could not cause decomposition like we see when an animal is hit by a vehicle and lies on the side of the road, or a tree falls to the ground and rots due to being exposed to the elements. The number of fossils found in dry, arid locations indicates that, at one time, those areas had to be completely submerged in water. Thus, the fossilization and the location where fossils are found support a global catastrophe, such as the flood in the days of Noah recorded in Genesis 7.

Medicine: When a male child is born today, he usually leaves the hospital in a few days if no health issues are preventing such. During those few days after birth, the parents will be allowed to decide whether they want their baby boy to be circumcised. If they decide they do, their child will be given a shot of Vitamin K before the surgery commences. That is because for blood clotting to occur, we know the human body must have high enough levels of prothrombin and vitamin K. Both are very low when a male child is first born; however, on the eighth day, both should occur at high enough levels naturally that the male child will be able to not continually bleed after surgery. We know this now because of scientific advancements; however, Moses wrote about this long ago in Genesis 17:12.

Fulfilled Prophecy: The Bible contains hundreds of prophecies that have been fulfilled with remarkable accuracy, including the birth (Mic. 5:2; Matt. 2:1), life (Zech. 9:9; Matt. 21:7-9), death (Isa. 53:7; Matt. 27: 12-14), and resurrection (Ps. 16:10; Acts 2:22) of Jesus Christ. Prophecies concerning nations and the scattering of people have also been fulfilled in detail (Deut. 28: 47-68; 2 Kings 17:24; 18:13; Isa. 13; Dan. 5:28). These prophecies demonstrate the divine inspiration of the Bible and provide a powerful witness to the truth of its message.

Archaeology: Excavations in the Middle East have uncovered numerous artifacts (Moabite Sone, Cyrus Cylinder) and structures (Sargon's Palace) that support the historical accuracy of the Bible. These include the discovery of the city of Jericho (which began in 1868 and continues today), which was destroyed just as the Bible describes, and the discovery of the Dead Sea Scrolls (1947-1956)[8], which contain copies of many of the books of the Old Testament. These and many other discoveries demonstrate the historical reliability of the Bible and provide robust evidence of its accuracy.

Cohesiveness of the Bible's Message: Despite being written over a period of 1400 years by 40 different authors, the Bible presents a consistent and unified message. The Bible teaches that God is love (1 John 4:8), that He desires a relationship with His people (2 Pet. 3:9), and that He has provided a way for us to be reconciled to Him through faith in Jesus Christ, including obedience to the Gospel (John 3:16-17; Rom. 1:16). This message of love and redemption is woven throughout the entire Bible, providing a powerful testimony to its truth and accuracy.

Geography/Topography: The Bible contains detailed descriptions of the geography and topography of the Middle East, including the locations of cities, rivers, and mountains. One example is in Luke 10:30-35, when Jesus described the man as *"going down from Jerusalem to Jericho."* Bible critics love to point out that Jerusalem is north of Jericho on a map; however, upon looking at a topographical map, one finds that Jerusalem is higher in elevation than Jericho. Thus, what Jesus said is true. These descriptions, along with others, have been confirmed by modern maps and archaeological discoveries, providing further evidence of the accuracy of the Bible.

Historical Writings: The Bible is not the only ancient text that describes events and people of the time. Other historical writings include those of Josephus, a Jewish historian born in 37-38

A.D. and died early in the second century. In his writing known as *Antiquities*, he references John the Baptist (Ant. 18.116ff.), James the Lord's brother (Ant. 20.200), and Jesus Christ (Ant. 18.63f)[9]. Roman historian Tacitus (56-118 A.D. is another such writer who corroborates the historical accuracy of the Bible. In Annals, he referred to the crucifixion of Jesus by order of Pontus Pilate: "Christus, the founder of the name [i.e., Christian], had undergone the death penalty in the reign of Tiberius, by sentence of the procurator Pontius Pilatus."[10] These writings provide further evidence of the accuracy of the Bible and its message.

CONCLUSION

Those early years when I was learning to drive in western Pennsylvania were foundational, especially when driving on ice and snow. I remember driving home one night in a blizzard so thick the headlights reflected off the falling snow, making it difficult to see. I've slid and skirted this way and that, and I've learned the tremendous value of making sure to pay attention and drive in such a way so your tires have the best opportunity to grip the road with good contact. To do so took a high level of determination and focus.

If you and I are determined to pay attention as the apostle Peter admonishes in 2 Peter 1:19, we must focus on the tires of our lives, making good contact with the road. Along with this, we must make sure we are on the right road. This is only accomplished when we are convinced paying attention is worth our time, the person telling us the direction to go is trustworthy, and the word we follow is the very Word of God, not some human interpretation.

REFLECTION

1. In your opinion, what does it mean to be determined to pay attention to the prophetic Word? What are some distractions that Satan often uses to make this more difficult?

2. What are some man-made philosophies and sayings that you have encountered and worked through as you continue to grow into the man God would have you to be?

3. How do you know whether a man can be trusted? What are some key indicators you look for? Are you a trustworthy man, and do others see you as such?

4. When someone tells you something and presents it as a fact, what process do you go through in your mind in dealing with or responding to such?

5. Do you believe the Bible is the inspired Word of God? If you do, why do you? If the answer is no, what would it take for you to be convinced the Bible is the inspired Word of God?

NOTES

CHAPTER 3
DETERMINED TO DO RIGHT

"Failure will never overtake me if my determination to succeed is strong enough."[1]

- Og Mandino -

Special Section: Synonyms of *determined*:

Intent—directed with strained or eager attention; having the mind, attention, or will concentrated on something or some end or purpose [2]

One of the critical traits of an intent person is his ability to stay focused. An intent person can block out distractions and stay on task, even when things get tough. This is an essential skill in today's fast-paced world, where distractions are everywhere. Being an intent person allows you to stay on track and accomplish your goals, even when the odds are against you.

Another important trait of intent people is their commitment to their goals. They are willing to put in the time and effort required to achieve their objectives, no matter how challenging. This type of commitment is essential for success, allowing you to push through obstacles and overcome adversity.

Another key trait of intent people is their ability to work hard and persevere. They understand that success is not always easy or immediate and that there will be setbacks and challenges. However, they are willing to work and keep pushing forward, even when things get tough.

Being an intent person means you are willing to step outside your comfort zone. You can't be rigid or inflexible, especially regarding your growth and approach to overcoming obstacles. This mindset is essential for growth and development, allowing you to learn new skills and discover new opportunities.

Being an intent person means being focused, committed, and willing to adapt to achieve your goals. It requires discipline and unrelenting perseverance. If you want to be successful, it is essential to cultivate this mindset. Your dedication and commitment can motivate others to pursue their goals and live purposeful lives.

HISTORICAL EXAMPLE

Henry Ford, the founder of the Ford Motor Company, is a name that is synonymous with success and innovation. However, many people do not know that Ford faced numerous failures and setbacks on his way to success. Despite these challenges, he remained determined and focused, eventually becoming one of the most successful entrepreneurs of his time.

He was born in 1863 to a family of farmers in a rural area of Michigan. Ford left his family's farm and moved to Detroit to work as an apprentice machinist at 16. He quickly became interested in the burgeoning automobile industry and began working for the Detroit Edison Company, which was developing electric cars. However, Ford was not content to work on other people's projects. He was determined to create his own automobile.

In 1899, Henry Ford founded his first automobile company, the Detroit Automobile Company. Unfortunately, it failed two years later due to financial difficulties and investor disagreements. Despite this setback, Ford did not abandon his dream of building a successful automobile company.

In 1903, Ford founded the Ford Motor Company with a group of investors. However, the company did not become an overnight success. It faced numerous challenges in its early years, including a shortage of capital and a lack of demand for automobiles. Ford was forced to borrow money to keep the company afloat, and he even went so far as to mortgage his own home to secure a loan.

His first car, the Model A, was not a success. However, Ford was undeterred and remained focused on his goal of creating an affordable, mass-produced automobile. In 1908, he introduced the Model T, the first affordable automobile for the average American. The Model T was an instant success, quickly becoming the best-selling car in the United States.

However, Ford's determination did not end with the success of the Model T. He was determined to make his car affordable for the average American. To do this, he had to streamline his manufacturing processes and reduce the cost of production. By 1913, he introduced the assembly line, allowing his workers to complete their tasks more quickly and efficiently. This not only reduced the cost of production but also allowed Ford to increase his workers' wages. This was a revolutionary idea at the time, and it helped to create a new middle class in America.

Ford's success was not without its challenges, however. In 1914, he faced a major setback when his workers went on strike. The strike lasted for six months, and it had a significant impact on the company's production and reputation. Ford responded by increasing wages for his workers and implementing other reforms, such as reducing the workday from nine hours to eight hours.

Despite these challenges, Ford's determination and vision led to his ultimate success, and it did not stop at his business ventures. He was also determined to make a difference in the world. He was a strong advocate of peace and a believer in the power of technology to improve people's lives. He created the Ford Foundation in 1936, which has since become one of the largest philanthropic organizations in the world.

Henry Ford's determination and drive to succeed in the automobile industry revolutionized manufacturing and changed the course of American history. His innovative ideas and approach to mass production have had a lasting impact on the economy and society. Ford's perseverance through failures and setbacks is a testament to his unwavering determination. His legacy as a business leader, philanthropist, and advocate for technology and education is a reminder of the power of determination and the impact one person can have on the world.[3,4]

I've always been interested in why people do what they do. I guess it's because I used to work at a group home for teenagers who had behavioral struggles in society. It's easiest to merely focus on the problem behaviors of children and seek to get them to stop the bad and do good. However, I've learned that there is always an underlying reason why someone does and thinks as he does. You can help them with their behavior struggles if you can discern that.

I'll never forget hearing the stories of mothers choosing random men over their children and the lasting negative impact that had on some of the boys. It's enough to break even a strong man's heart to see a teenager who has struggled in life work the recovery program in place for them to earn a visit on Sunday with their family only to hear that the boy's mother or father never showed up because they had something better to do or someone else with whom they preferred to spend the day. That boy comes back to the home broken. Why should he try? If he's not shown love and attention by those who are supposed to love him the most, he will act out and try to get any attention possible.

I've heard and seen the impact of stories that would make most cringe. There are stories of parents allowing their sons to be sexually abused in the back room while they were getting high or drunk in the front of the house. I've seen scars on the arms of a boy whose father used to put cigarettes out on them, leaving a permanent reminder of the pain caused by those who were supposed to nurture and protect him. I've even seen mothers try to buy their way into the lives of their sons with expensive shoes and clothes, all the while emphasizing to those boys that "love" (which really was not love but a mother feeling guilty for her behavior) can be bought and sold just as a pair of shoes. What impact will that have on their future relationships?

In all these and countless other scenarios, the truth that a person always has a reason for doing what they do reverberates. The older I get, the more that lesson has been etched in my mind. In ministry, I've seen men wrapped up in pornographic addictions melt when they acknowledge what's really going on behind the scenes. A son whose father always told him he wasn't good enough runs to find someone who will. A husband who is broken because his marriage is filled with unhealthy criticism at every turn seeks acceptance in "the arms of a woman" on a video. An employee finds the stress of his job too much to bear, so he seeks what he thinks is relief in the comfort of a woman on the screen of his phone. I've seen it. Men who are broken or hurt are addicted to pornography as a coping mechanism; only the behavior doesn't help them. They find themselves more hurt, and the wake of pain they leave behind destroys those around them.

In all, the reality is that we are still accountable for our actions, regardless of the reason we did them. We emphasized that to those boys in the group home. We told them that they can't control the behaviors of others, but they are in control of their response. They didn't have to choose a harmful and destructive path in life just because other people struggled and failed in their journey. The same can be said for the man addicted to pornography because he is coping with something in his life. It can also be said to the man who looks at me in the mirror. We don't have to choose negative behaviors just because we are hurt or desire something. We are in control of our actions, and we are accountable for our actions.

The Old Testament prophet Ezekiel said it this way when he wrote concerning the judgment of God,

> *Yet you say, "Why should the son not bear the punishment for the father's iniquity?" When the son has practiced justice and righteousness and has observed all My statutes and done them, he shall surely live. The person who sins will die. The son will not bear the punishment for the father's iniquity, nor will the father bear the punishment for the son's iniquity; the righteousness of the righteous will be upon himself, and the wickedness of the wicked will be upon himself. "But if the wicked man turns from all his sins which he has committed and observes all My statutes and practices justice and righteousness, he shall surely live; he shall not die. All his transgressions which he has committed will not be remembered against him; because of his righteousness which he has practiced, he will live. Do I have any pleasure in the death of the wicked," declares the Lord God, "rather than that he should turn from his ways and live?"* (Ezek. 18: 19-23)

Since the person who does the actions will be judged for the action, it stands to reason that each of us has a choice regarding our actions. After all, a loving God doesn't judge us for something we can't control. On the other hand, a righteous Judge cannot sit back and not hold individuals who do wrong accountable. So, we must all swallow the fact that we are in control of our actions; therefore, we get to choose them. If we are determined to do right, vital values and critical elements must be present.

In 2 Peter 2, we are introduced to the actions and motivations of the *"false prophets"* who bask in greed and sensuality. Their lifestyle is rooted in the very denial of the Master who bought them (v. 1) and a belief that an eternal judgment will not happen (3:3-4). These, who once had escaped the defilements of the world, have now become trapped in them once again (2:20). Both their message and their actions indicate this horrific state (2:21). Their belief and motivations dictate their actions, and they will be held accountable for their sins (2:3, 9).

We want to avoid their way of life and the inevitable ending. But how will we do so? We must not walk in their footprints, but we can learn from them by observing where they ventured off the trail. We can set our minds to do right instead of giving in to every passion or potential motivating factor that has come our way in the past or will in the future. It will take severe intent and determination to do right; however, the reward waiting at the end of the journey is more than worth it. It's beyond anything these or any other "false prophets" promise.

DISCUSSION

To be a person determined to do right…

1) I Must Value the Way of Truth

In life, some things are just bigger than you and me. A soldier who is sent into battle knows an objective must be accomplished. He will prepare himself physically and mentally to the best of his ability. The military will equip him with the best technology and defenses to ensure the mission is accomplished and his life is spared. With all the scenarios they can think of mapped out ahead of time, it's inevitable that something will occur on the mission that was outside of the plan. It's also very likely the soldier may lay down his life, knowing the importance of accomplishing the mission. The mission is bigger than any one of the soldiers.

Another instance where something is larger than any one individual is when it comes to sports. Everybody loves positive press, and to get their name in the headlines for a wonderful accomplishment, at times, can drive actions. A quarterback seeking the record for most passing yards in a season may call an audible and throw more than the coach initially intended. If he catches so many passes or has a certain number of total yards in a single season, a receiver with a significant financial bonus on the line might let his frustration known to the coach, quarterback, team, and the media. The whole squad fails when a person becomes so wrapped up in his success that he quits functioning as a single part of the bigger picture. The team and winning as such is more significant than any one person, even if it means benching your starting quarterback or receiver because he isn't performing at a high level during that specific game.

More important than both of the previous illustrations is the bigger picture of the will of God. In his first letter to the scattered Christians, Peter stressed the importance of their new birth (1:3, 23). This new birth meant they were living for a different cause and purpose, much bigger than any of them. In chapter 2, Peter stressed that they were living stones being built up as *"a spiritual house for a holy priesthood, to offer up spiritual sacrifices acceptable to God through Jesus Christ"* (v. 5). He later told them they were the holy priesthood (v. 9); thus, instructing them as a holy people to live differently than the rest of those around them (vv. 11-13). This was so that they would not *"wage war against their own soul"* (v. 11), and so those who were seeking their harm might *"glorify God in the day of visitation"* (v. 12).

The bigger picture is that God wants all souls in Heaven with Him, even if it means you and I must encounter challenging and life-threatening situations during our stay on this earth (1 Pet. 3:17). In his second letter, Peter emphasizes this point even more clearly when he writes, *"The Lord is not slow about His promise, as some count slowness, but is patient toward you not wishing for any to perish but for all to come to repentance"* (2 Pet. 3:9). That's the good news of the Gospel. God does love the world so much so that He gave His only begotten Son, Jesus Christ, to die on the cross for our sins (John 3:16-17). He raised Him from the grave after three days in the tomb (1 Cor. 15:1-4), so you and I have a living hope (1 Pet. 1:3). This hope is available to the entire world. God has set it up so you and I, as disciples of Jesus Christ, would go with this saving message to our friends, family members, co-workers, neighbors, and beyond to bring others to Him (Matt. 28:19-20).

The *"way of truth,"* as Peter calls it in 2 Peter 2:2, is so important. Consider a lengthy list of Scriptures explaining what the Bible says regarding truth and the impact this has on one's eternal salvation.

- Psalm 25:10—*"All the paths of the Lord are lovingkindness and **truth** to those who keep His covenant and His testimonies."*

- Psalm 31:5—*"Into Your hand I commit my spirit; You have ransomed me, O Lord, God of **truth**."*

- Psalm 86:11—*"Teach me Your way, O Lord; I will walk in Your **truth**; Unite my heart to fear Your name."*

- John 1:14—*"And the Word became flesh, and dwelt among us, and we saw His glory, glory as of the only begotten from the Father, full of grace and **truth**."*

- John 1:17—*"For the Law was given through Moses; grace and **truth** were realized through Jesus Christ."*

- John 8:31-32—*"So Jesus was saying to those Jews who had believed Him, 'If you continue in My word, then you are truly disciples of Mine; and you will know the **truth**, and the **truth** will make you free.'"*

- John 14:6—*"Jesus said to him, 'I am the way, and the **truth**, and the life; no one comes to the Father but through Me.'"*

- John 17:17—*"Sanctify them in the **truth**; Your word is **truth**."*

- Romans 1:18—*"For the wrath of God is revealed from heaven against all ungodliness and unrighteousness of men who suppress the **truth** in unrighteousness."*

- Romans 2:5-8—*"But because of your stubbornness and unrepentant heart you are storing up wrath for yourself in the day of wrath and revelation of the righteous judgment of God, who will render to each person according to his deeds: to those who by perseverance in doing good seek for glory and honor and immortality, eternal life; but to those who are selfishly ambitious and do not obey the **truth**, but obey unrighteousness, wrath and indignation."*

- Ephesians 1:13—*"In Him, you also, after listening to the message of **truth**, the gospel of your salvation—having also believed, you were sealed in Him with the Holy Spirit of promise."*

- Ephesians 4:17-24—*"So this I say, and affirm together with the Lord, that you walk no longer just as the Gentiles also walk, in the futility of their mind, being darkened in their understanding, excluded from the life of God because of the ignorance that is in them, because of the hardness of their heart; and they, having become callous, have given themselves over to sensuality for the practice of every kind of impurity with greediness. But you did not learn Christ in this way, if indeed you have heard Him and have been taught in Him, just as* **truth** *is in Jesus, that, in reference to your former manner of life, you lay aside the old self, which is being corrupted in accordance with the lusts of deceit, and that you be renewed in the spirit of your mind, and put on the new self, which in the likeness of God has been created in righteousness and holiness of the* **truth**.*"*

- *1 Timothy 2:3*—*"This is good and acceptable in the sight of God our Savior, who desires all men to be saved and to come to the knowledge of the* **truth**.*"*

- *2 Timothy 4:3-4*—*"For the time will come when they will not endure sound doctrine; but wanting to have their ears tickled, they will accumulate for themselves teachers in accordance to their own desires, and will turn away their ears from the* **truth** *and will turn aside to myths."*

While not an exhaustive listing of all the verses in the Bible that address the concept of truth, from this, we can clearly see the immense value of the way of truth. Truth is rooted in the very nature of God and is made known to man in Jesus Christ. It can set us free from the wages of sin and death and should change how we live in this world. The way of truth is revealed to us through the preaching of the Gospel and leads to eternal hope. While God wants all men to know the truth, not everyone will love it and want to follow its lit path. Some will abandon the truth, preferring myths or cleverly devised tales, as Peter addresses in 2 Peter 1:16. Sadly, because of their influence, they will lead others down the same condemned path as they malign, bring blasphemy or demean, the way of truth (2 Pet. 2:2). The result for these and those who follow them will be condemnation. Not because God is not love, but because in rejecting and bringing blaspheme on the way of truth, they have attacked the very nature of God and His saving work in Christ Jesus.

That's why if we are going to be people who are determined to do right, we must first value the way of truth. When we do, everything we do in life will be weighed against what impact it will have on the way of truth, our journey along the way, and the influence we have on others to either walk on the path or veer away. I want to do right, not because I want my name in the headlines. Instead, I want God's name "in the headlines" as my life is lived as a sacrifice before Him. The way of truth is more significant than you and me, and if we are going to do right, we must not simply acknowledge that fact. We must value that truth.

2) I Must Hold Fast to the Right Way

Logic tells us that if there is a right way, by default there must be a wrong way. This is true because you can't have right without the opposite existing. It's like knowing what hot water is without knowing that cold water exists—or understanding light without a grasp of darkness. Some concepts can only exist in pairs; thus, a wrong way must exist when there is a right way. This is true because the idea of comparison is inherently built into these words. Right, as compared to what? Hot water as weighed against what? Light by comparison to what measurement? In all these, a standard must exist and stand as the measurement by which all these are compared.

In 2 Peter 2:15, when talking about the false prophets (2:1), we read, "*forsaking* **the right way**, *they have gone astray, having followed the way of Balaam, the son of Beor, who loved the wages of unrighteousness*" (emp. added). Since a "*right way*" exists, there must be a wrong way. That's the point Peter is making. These false prophets are accused of "*forsaking*," meaning "to cause to be left in a place, leave (behind)," and have "*gone astray*," meaning "to proceed without a sense of proper direction, go astray, be misled, wander about aimlessly."[6] Ironically, this means they once were on the right way, and like sheep who wander and chase what they believe to be greener pastures, they have left the fold, leaving the protection of the shepherd, and are now choosing to be exposed to the wolves and countless other dangers that are present in the wild. The problem is they have conditioned themselves to this end. Peter says they are like *"unreasoning animals, born as creatures of instinct to be captured and killed"* (2:12).

What a sad and terrifying state to be in! However, they don't care. Peter reveals that these purveyors of perversion "revel" in the daytime meaning (2:13), a word meaning *"engagement in a fast, self-indulgent lifestyle, indulgence, reveling."*[7] They choose wrong and blatantly engage in actions consistent with that choice in front of everyone. That's what Peter refers to as *"the way of Balaam, the son of Beor"* (2:15). While the original audience would have undoubtedly understood this very well, it will do us good to revisit this account in Numbers 22–24. However, we will benefit even more by investigating the opposite of *"the way of Balaam"* as well. After all, since Peter is drawing a comparison between "the right way" and *"the way of Balaam,"* you and I can gain a fuller understanding and appreciation if we study both. Consider the following.

A. The Way of Balaam (Numbers 22–24):

> *Forsaking the right way, they have gone astray, having followed* ***the way of Balaam****, the son of Beor, who loved the wages of unrighteousness; but he received a rebuke for his own transgression, for a mute donkey, speaking with a voice of a man, restrained the madness of the prophet.* (2 Pet. 2:15-16, emp. added)

Balaam is most notably the prime example from the Old Testament used by New Testament authors Peter and Jude to explain a core motivating problem with the false teachers of their day. Being known to Balak king of Moab as a prophet/divinator, Balaam was sought to curse Israel as they camped in the plains of Moab. Much wealth and honor were promised to him; however, the Bible records that God came to Balaam and asked, *"Who are these men with you?"* (Num. 22:9). Balaam explained the situation; however, God made it very clear that he was not to go with these men nor was he to curse the Israelites (v. 12).

As we read of Balaam reporting this to the entourage Balak sent (v. 13), we are almost left with a sense that Balaam's submission and obedience to God, his resolve in the face of an offer of significant financial gain, was destined to serve as a very positive and good example throughout time. However, when the men returned a second time, many more people who were in greater positions of influence and power with them. They sought Balaam's services again, only this time, there was a promise of even greater wealth and gain (v. 17).

Balaam should have said something like, "I already told you 'No.' Now leave!" However, as the New Testament reveals (2 Pet. 2:15; Jude 11), Balaam's internal greed drove him to entertain the idea and even beseech God (Num. 22:19-20). God had already told him "No" once; however, He will not stop Balaam from making his own decisions. So, God commands Balaam to go but to obey only the word and speak the word God gives him.

God would not allow Balaam to curse the Israelites; however, for Balaam, the damage was already done. Everything Balaam said sounded good: "*Though Balak were to give me his house full of silver and gold, I could not do anything, either small or great, contrary to the command of the Lord my God*" (v. 18). It seemed he was going to do the right thing, but God is not only interested in doing the right thing. He's interested in His disciples doing the right thing for the right reasons, and Balaam's reasons were greed-filled and abhorrent before God.

Thus, God sends an angel with a sword to stand in the way of Balaam's donkey. The donkey can see him, but Balaam is spiritually blinded. Out of anger and because his vision is clouded with greed, Balaam strikes the donkey three times until finally, the donkey is given a voice (v. 28). In verse 31, we see a crucial moment in this narrative when the Bible says, "*Then the Lord opened the eyes of Balaam, and he saw the angel of the Lord standing in the way with his drawn sword in his hand; and he bowed all the way to the ground*" (v. 31). A man who, like a wild animal, was driven by greed is now bowing to the ground because his eyes have been opened.

Like Balaam, the false prophets Peter writes of in his second letter have hearts filled with greed and eyes continually lusting after what is forbidden (2 Pet. 2:14). There's never enough to satisfy their sinful appetite, so they continue to deceive, exploit, and entice weaker individuals, perhaps young in their faith, to follow them. They are blind and desire others to join them in their unrepentant and pitiful existence, promising the world but ensuring damnation.

B. The Right Way (Noah and Lot)

> *Forsaking the **right way**, they have gone astray, having followed the way of Balaam, the son of Beor, who loved the wages of unrighteousness.* (2 Pet. 2:15; emp. added)

To draw a stark contrast between the righteous, those who walk according to the way of truth (v. 2), and the unrighteousness of those who walk in like manner as that of the false prophets in chapter 2, Peter highlights two key individuals from the Old Testament: Noah and Lot (vv. 5, 7). Both individuals lived in challenging cultural contexts. However, both made a determined decision not to be absorbed by the sensual saturation and self-seeking normative behavior of their day.

Noah, a preacher of righteousness (v. 5), is described as one who found favor in the eyes of the Lord (Gen. 6:8), being a righteous man, blameless in his time, and one who walked with God (Gen. 6:9). He is also described as being seen by God to be the only one in his time to be righteous (Gen. 7:1). While not being a perfect man who had lacked need for the grace of God (Rom. 3:23), Noah is remembered as one who boldly proclaimed what was right and just according to God. However, he didn't simply preach the sermon. He lived the sermon in a time when *"the earth was corrupt in the sight of God, and the earth was filled with violence"* (Gen. 6:11). It was God's observation that all those who inhabited the earth had chased after corruption and gained the outcome of such (Gen. 6:12). At first glance, all these descriptions may not stand out to the casual reader; however, upon closer examination, one can't help but see that as bad as the corruption had gotten—demonstrated by the just response of God in causing a global flood—the righteousness found in Noah was just as significant.

Like Noah, Lot lived during a time of tremendous and disgusting circumstances. By choice, Lot moved his family and herds to the valley of the Jordan, which would have included Sodom (Gen. 13:10-11). He made his selection based on the beauty of the land and the abundant resources; however, he should have investigated the moral standards by which those in this valley operated.

While Noah is described explicitly in the Scriptures in specific ways depicting the reasons he is included in 2 Peter, Lot is not. His being included by Peter seems to be based upon his actions (inviting the messengers to stay at his house and refusing to hand the men over to the men of the city) that reveal his character. When we read the account of the destruction of the cities of Sodom and Gomorrah, these actions communicate a distinction between him and the land's inhabitants. Above this, upon observing the dialogue between the Lord and Abraham in Genesis 18 regarding any righteous who dwell in Sodom, one can conclude a connection exists between them and Lot's being included by Peter as *"righteous Lot"* (2 Pet. 2:7).

It's fascinating to see the distinguishable "ways" Peter is describing. If we are determined to do right, we can't stand silently at the crossroads of Balaam and the right way. The false prophets and those who followed their way of greed and sensuality made their choice. Thus, they will end up where that road leads. However, the depth of sorrow in this passage is realized when one stops to consider these who Peter describes as *"stains and blemishes"* (2 Pet. 2:13), were once washed as white as snow, having been *"bought"* by the Master (2 Pet. 2:1) before they forsook the right way (2 Pet. 2:15). In other words, they didn't have to end up the way Peter describes them. They did so because they did not hold fast to the right way.

3) I Must Cherish the Freedom

Of all the descriptions of people that should cause the greatest sorrow, a person once having escaped the defilements of the flesh only to turn back and become entangled in the very way of life that separates them from God is at the top of the list. Poor money management skills are not good; however, it's not damnable. Not having the knowledge to work on your vehicle may be an expensive position, but it will not cost you on the day of judgment. Not being the best student, the best athlete, or even the best-looking person may be impactful to some on this earth; however, none of these matter in eternity. What does matter is whether one holds fast to the hand of Jesus in continued submission to the will of God. That's why the one who knows the joy of escape and turns back to the destitute of enslavement is the saddest of them all.

When we consider what the Bible says regarding the transition in the eternal standing of a person who obeys the way of truth, the terrible magnitude of the decision to turn back to sin weighs heavy. Think about the beautiful state of the person who has been set free from the bondage of sin.

- Romans 5:9—*"Much more then, having now been **justified** by His blood, we shall be saved from the wrath of God through Him."*

- Romans 5:11—*"And not only this, but we also exult in God through our Lord Jesus Christ, through whom we have now **received the reconciliation**."*

- Ephesians 2:4-5—*"But God, being rich in mercy, because of His great love with which He loved us, even when we were dead in our transgressions, **made us alive** together with Christ."*

- Colossians 2:13—*"When you were dead in your transgressions and the uncircumcision of your flesh, He **made you alive** together with Him, having **forgiven** us all our transgressions."*

- 1 Corinthians 6:11—*"Such were some of you; but you were **washed**, but you were sanctified, but you were **justified** in the name of the Lord Jesus Christ and in the Spirit of our God."*

Peter claims the ones who have, in "obedience to the truth, purified their souls" (1 Pet. 1:22), have a hopeful expectation of an "inheritance which is imperishable and undefiled and will not fade away, reserved in heaven" (1 Pet. 1:4). So, when contemplating the response of the false prophets in 2 Peter, we are left dumbfounded by their decision to chase after temporary pleasures and forfeit the favor of God. However, that's precisely what they did.

But why? Why did they turn back, like a dog returning to its vomit (2 Pet. 2:22)? Why would anyone, after having tasted the kindness of the Lord (1 Pet. 2:3), want to taste the filth of sin? The answer we find in 2 Peter 2 is what we must guard against if we are determined to do right.

In returning to verse 15, where Peter used Balaam as an example in discussing the contrary way, he said Balaam "*loved the wages of unrighteousness.*" The word *loved* is the Greek word *agapao* and is defined here as "to have high esteem for or satisfaction with something, take pleasure in."[8] It's the same word used in John 3:19 when we read, "*This is the judgment, that the Light has come into the world, and men **loved** the darkness rather than the Light, for their deeds were evil*" (emp. added). In both verses, the key is that value was assigned and actions followed.

What a person values will genuinely impact the way they live. If we value our desires above being in a right relationship with God, our lives will reflect this sad reality. Ultimately, that's what the lives of the false prophets of 2 Peter display. Their wrong thinking about the second coming of Jesus (2 Pet. 3:3-4) and their love for the wages of unrighteousness unleashed a beast of passion and self-pursuit. Their every thought was for their fulfillment and satisfaction.

CONCLUSION

There are always reasons behind behaviors. If we are determined to do right, our reasons must be worth the sacrifices we are called to make. People who desire to compete in the Summer Olympics must work hard to train their bodies and hone their skills. Often, it takes a lifetime of commitment to compete in a race that will take a few minutes or less. That's a lot of work for a short competition. However, to the determined athlete, this dedicated lifestyle is entirely worth the sacrifices because they know a great reward is at the finish line.

To those sowing to the flesh, our choice to deny the temporary benefits of sin doesn't make sense. When desire is rooted in only what this life can bring, to forgo unrestrained passions is pointless. However, for those sowing to the spirit and who genuinely know the kindness of God, nothing on this earth is worth the exchange of our souls. That's why we must determine now to do right. We must value the way of truth, hold fast to the right way, and cherish the freedom we have in Christ Jesus.

If we are determined to do right, we must value the freedom we have in Christ Jesus more than we love ungodly, temporary feelings of pleasure here on this earth. In obeying the Gospel, we have died to ourselves (Matt. 16: 24-25; Gal. 2:20). This fact means we are now living for the will of God, daily choosing to leave the old man of sin in the grave.

REFLECTION

1. How does motivation develop in a person's life, and why is it a significant factor in human behavior?

2. We value what we find to be important to us. Why is truth to be valued? Why is the Truth and the Way of Truth something to be valued? Do you value the Way of Truth in your life? How do you know?

3. In this chapter, we clearly see the stark contrast between the "way of Balaam" and the "right way." Knowing how different these paths are, what are some of the reasons a man would forsake the right way and go the way of Balaam? What advice would you give to another man to avoid these pitfalls?

4. After tasting the Lord's kindness, why would anyone want to return to the filth of sin?

5. Do you agree or disagree with this statement: "What a person values will genuinely impact the way they live?" Why or why not? How do you develop values that will help you get in your walk with the Lord and with those in your life?

NOTES

CHAPTER 4
DETERMINED TO BE RIGHT

"Determination is the wake-up call to the human will."[1]

- Tony Robbins -

Special Section: Synonyms of *determined*:

Adamant—**sticking to an opinion, purpose, or course of action in spite of reason, arguments, or persuasion.**[2]

While some may view this trait as stubbornness or inflexibility, being adamant can have many benefits. When you are determined and persistent, you are more likely to stick to your plans and see them through to completion. You are less likely to give up when faced with obstacles or setbacks and more likely to find creative solutions to problems. This determination can be beneficial in achieving long-term goals in life and when thinking about your eternal goal of heaven.

Being an adamant person can also boost self-confidence. You are less likely to be held back by fear or self-doubt and more likely to seize opportunities when they arise. This confidence can benefit personal and professional relationships, as it can help you assert yourself and communicate effectively.

Being an adamant person can also lead to more tremendous success and achievement. When you are determined and persistent, you are more likely to put in the time and effort required to excel in your pursuits. Whether it's a new hobby, a new skill in your career, or, most importantly, your spiritual growth, being an adamant person can help you achieve greater success than less persistent ones.

Ultimately, being adamant is about being authentic and diligently seeking to achieve your goals while growing along the way. It is a balance between persistence and flexibility, requiring self-awareness and a willingness to learn from successes and failures. When this quality is one you possess, it's challenging to be deterred, and that is crucial for all who desire to excel in their pursuits, both in this life and in the one to come.

HISTORICAL EXAMPLE

Walt Disney is a name that is synonymous with creativity and imagination. He is the man behind one of the most successful entertainment companies in the world, and his legacy continues to inspire generations of people. But many people don't know the story behind Walt Disney's success and the determination and resolve he displayed throughout his life.

In Chicago, Illinois, Walter "Walt" Elias Disney was born on December 5, 1901. From a young age, he had a passion for drawing and spent much of his childhood creating cartoons and sketches. However, his childhood was not an easy one. His family struggled financially, and he had to work odd jobs to support himself.

Despite these challenges, Walt never gave up his dream of becoming an artist. He attended the Academy of Fine Arts in Chicago but dropped out after one year to pursue his passion for animation. He moved to California and started his animation studio, which he called Laugh-O-Gram.

The studio was initially successful, but it soon faced financial difficulties. Walt was forced to file for bankruptcy in 1923 and lost everything he had worked so hard for. However, he didn't let this setback stop him. He packed his bags and moved to Hollywood, where he started working on his next project.

Walt's next project was a cartoon character called Oswald the Lucky Rabbit. He created the character and sold it to a distributor, but he soon realized he had made a mistake. The distributor had taken ownership of the character and had hired Walt's animators to work on it without his permission.

Walt was devastated by this loss, but he didn't give up. He knew he needed to create a new character he could call his own. That character was Mickey Mouse. Walt began crafting the character of Mickey Mouse in 1927, and in 1928, "Steamboat Willie," an early cartoon equipped with voices and music, was released. Mickey Mouse and Walt Disney both quickly became sensations. The character's success allowed Walt to build his animation studio, which he called Disney Studios.

Disney Studios was a massive success, and Walt continued to create new characters and movies that captured the hearts of audiences worldwide. However, his success was not without its challenges. He faced numerous setbacks and obstacles throughout his life but never let them stop him.

Walt faced one of the most significant challenges during World War II. The war substantially impacted the entertainment industry, and Disney Studios was no exception. Walt was forced to halt production on many of his projects, and he even had to loan money to his employees to help them through tough times.

Despite these challenges, Walt never gave up. He continued to work tirelessly on his projects and even created a series of propaganda films to support the war effort. His dedication and hard work paid off, and Disney Studios emerged from the war more robust than ever.

Ultimately, Walt Disney is remembered in history as one who displayed incredible determination and resolve throughout his life. He faced numerous challenges, but he never let them stop him. His passion for animation and storytelling inspired generations, and his legacy continues today. Walt Disney is a true inspiration to anyone who has ever faced a setback or obstacle in their life, and his story is a reminder that anything is possible with hard work and determination.³

There is a big difference between "looking right" and "being right." Unfortunately, in a time inundated with social media likes and portrayals of our ideal selves, this distinction gets lost easily. One is selfishly concerned with what everybody else thinks about them, and the other is concerned only with what God sees in them. One is only interested in going through the motions; the other is dedicated to making sure his character and motivation are in alignment so that his deeds are an overflow of his steadfast devotion to God. Perhaps the most significant difference between these two is one has a firm conviction that who he is before God is more important than how others perceive him. It's not that the person who desires to "be right" is not concerned with his influence on others. However, where he excels is understanding and accepting that God is the only Judge, and one day, all of humanity will be held accountable for the deeds done in the flesh (2 Cor. 5:10).

I think the character in Hollywood history that best summarizes the difference between the two is Eddy Haskell from the show *Leave It to Beaver*. With a smooth compliment, Eddy always appeared to be a nice boy in front of the adults. However, when the parents weren't within hearing distance, he schemed and talked down about people, especially the Beaver. His desire to "look right" only served his overall purpose of manipulating the perception others held regarding him and ultimately served to advance his selfishness.

In 2 Peter, the false prophets represent the Eddy Haskells of Peter's time. They are self-seeking and driven by the lusts of the flesh. They have smooth tongues that make grand promises; however, they are *"springs without water and mists driven by a storm"* (2 Pet. 2:17). With greed as their driver, they present a message both in word and example of sensuality and debauchery. Unfortunately, their "looking right" captivates the spiritually immature (2 Pet. 2:18) as they constantly dig their own grave of enslavement and corruption. However, as the letter advances to chapter 3, we clearly see that's not the way God desires His true disciples to be. Instead, God demands "being right."

Why is this the case? The answer is simple: because Jesus is coming back, and when He does, it will not be favorable for those who spent their life sowing to the lusts of the flesh as these false prophets have done. On that day, the secrets of men will be judged by God through Christ Jesus (Rom. 2:16). The stubborn and unrepentant hearts have nothing but the expectation of wrath and revelation on that dreadful day (Rom. 2:5). However, for those who have loved the way of righteousness, a crown of righteousness awaits and will be awarded on that day by the righteous Judge (2 Tim. 4:8).

The false prophets did not accept this simple truth. Instead, they argued that because Jesus had not returned according to their expected timetable, He must not be coming, and the whole concept of a Judgment Day was a farce (2 Peter 3:3-4). By their logic, since there was no Judgment Day, there was no accountability for the way they lived, so fulfilling their lustful desires was their objective, and "looking right" served to trap the weak. Their wrong thinking about the second coming of Jesus led to evil and sinful behavior.

In chapter 3, Peter explains that he is writing, "*stirring up your sincere mind by way of reminder*" (2 Pet. 3:1), regarding what they have been taught about the coming of the Lord and what kind of people they are to be while they eagerly await His coming. He also stated this desire earlier in chapter 1:13. His desire to awaken these Christians and ensure they are not asleep serves as the springboard to the instruction we find in this chapter regarding our lives. While, as disciples of Jesus Christ, we want to be "light" and "salt" in this world (Matt. 5:13-16), we do not let the way others talk about us drive us. Instead, in allowing the way of truth to be our path and the light of the Word of God to serve as our light (Ps. 119:105), we seek to "be right" before God.

But what does that mean specifically in 2 Peter 3? Consider these five key characteristics Peter by inspiration of the Holy Spirit highlights and urges these Christians to adopt as they await the return of our Lord and Savior.

DISCUSSION

1) Be Holy in Conduct and Godliness

In Leviticus 19:2, we read of God commanding Moses to speak to the sons of Israel and say to them, *"You shall be holy, for I the Lord your God am holy."* Having set their eyes on the promised land of Canaan, the children of God were unaware of all that awaited them. I don't mean they didn't have knowledge of the false gods of the people who were currently inhabiting the land or that they hadn't heard stories and myths of lifestyles that involved not just unrestrained sexual lust but also child sacrifice. I'm referring to the difficulty of being drawn into a similar lifestyle. The strong magnetic pull of a culture that normalized sinful behavior and the tendency of humanity to rationalize and justify why going along with the cultural context in which we find ourselves planted is captivating. It's easier, and God, knowing this to be accurate, wanted to make a bold statement regarding His expectations.

The above-quoted verse tends to focus on the first part, *"You shall be holy,"* and we will allow the text to explain what that meant for them in their time and what it meant for us in ours as well. However, if we are going to grasp the first part of that statement entirely, we must completely appreciate the second part. In Leviticus 18–20, we read no less than 25 times where God says, *"I am the Lord"* or *"I am the Lord your God."* While having a scholarly knowledge of Hebrew and Greek is undoubtedly a blessing, it's unnecessary in this case. When a statement or a point is made this many times in a relatively short section of Scripture, it's evident that the author intends for a point to be implanted in the readers' minds and serve as the backbone for instruction.

The concept of God being their Lord and the call for that to mean a significant amount in their lives predates the events in the book of Leviticus. We can venture back to the book of Exodus 20:1-6 when Moses was on Mt. Sinai, receiving the covenant commandments from God, and see this same point of emphasis serving as the anchor or the "Why?" behind the behavior and character God expects.

> *Then God spoke all these words, saying, "**I am the Lord your God**, who brought you out of the land of Egypt, out of the house of slavery. You shall have no other gods before Me. You shall not make for yourself an idol, or any likeness of what is in heaven above or on the earth beneath or in the water under the earth. You shall not worship them or serve them; for I, **the Lord your God**, am a jealous God, visiting the iniquity of the fathers on the children, on the third and the fourth generations of those who hate Me, but showing lovingkindness to thousands, to those who love Me and keep My commandments."* (emp. added)

In this covenant language, we see the goodness of God displayed in His rescuing the people from bondage, the kindness of God allowing a covenant relationship with Him, and the expectation of God that being in covenant with Him means their behaviors and—more importantly—their lives were to reflect their devotion to Him. However, even this event on Mt. Sinai is not the first time we see this reasoning established.

In Genesis 17: 1-8, we read,

> *Now when Abram was ninety-nine years old, the Lord appeared to Abram and said to him, "I am God Almighty; Walk before Me, and be blameless. I will establish My covenant between Me and you, And I will multiply you exceedingly." Abram fell on his face, and God talked with him, saying, "As for Me, behold, My covenant is with you, And you will be the father of a multitude of nations. No longer shall your name be called Abram, But your name shall be Abraham; For I have made you the father of a multitude of nations. I will make you exceedingly fruitful, and I will make nations of you, and kings will come forth from you. I will establish My covenant between Me and you and your descendants after you throughout their generations for an everlasting covenant, **to be God to you and to your descendants after you**. I will give to you and to your descendants after you, the land of your sojournings, all the land of Canaan, for an everlasting possession; and I will be their God."* (emp. added)

Even during the early period of the call of Abraham and the promises God made regarding multiplying his descendants and an extraordinary land that would be given to them, there was an anchor that held fast. That anchor served, and still does today, to cement and root the reasons God expects His people to be and act differently than the world. If we claim to be children of God, being in covenant with Him through the blood of His Son, then our lives and the motivation at our very core should reflect such.

That's the backbone of why God told Moses what He did in Exodus 20 and the children of Israel in Leviticus 18–20. In each case, the behavior God expects from His people flows from a covenant relationship with Him. That changes everything about the person. When God is your God, that means something beyond merely "going through the motions" or doing good to get good in return. That's where the hypocrites in Matthew 6 displayed a disconnect. They were doing good to get the good that man would give them. They looked the part while being displeasing to God throughout the entire exercise. That is because the true child of God practices holiness in his conduct and has godly reverence and awe because he undoubtedly understands who God is and the tremendous, overwhelming blessing that comes with being in covenant with Him.

That's why what Peter writes in 2 Peter 3:11 when he says, *"What sort of people ought you to be in holy conduct and godliness?"* is so important. Peter's not asking a question. Instead, he's making a definitive statement based upon the incredible realities of God that the false teachers are denying but remain sound and trustworthy.

- (v. 5) The Power of God Has Been Displayed in His Speaking Creation into Existence.
- (v. 6) The Judgment of God Has Been Realized with the Onset of the Flood.
- (v. 9) The Patience of God Remains Strong in That He Desires All to Come to Repentance.
- (v. 10) The Promise of God Regarding the Day of the Lord is Going to Place Both His Power and Judgment on Display Once Again.

Since this is certain and the evidence is plain, the one who truly loves and reveres Him will intentionally and deliberately respond to reflect this conviction.

"*Holy conduct*" means a lifestyle that is "pure, perfect, worthy of God."[4] "*Godliness*" encompasses an "awesome respect accorded to God, devoutness, piety, godliness."[5] Both entail purpose, intent, determination, and sacrifice. At their core, these are not merely going through the motions of doing right. Even hypocrites can "do right." However, if these qualities and the display of such are to be, one must be right.

2) Be Looking and Hastening for the Day

Expectations influence preparations. Think about it. If you know you're going on a car trip tomorrow with the family, you will spend time preparing for that trip. If you expect it to be cold, you will prepare accordingly. If you're going to stay in the mountains, it wouldn't make much sense to pack for the beach. What you expect influences the preparations you make.

Now consider what your life is like when you live every day "*looking for*," "to give thought to something that is viewed as lying in the future, wait for, look for, expect"[6], and "*hastening for*" "to cause something to happen or come into being by exercising special effort,"[7] the day of the Lord's return. For starters, don't think "*looking*" and "*hastening*" for the day of the Lord's return means that you stand outside looking up at the sky all the time just trying to catch the first glimpse of the smoke from the fire (2 Thess. 1:7). That would be rather pointless because the description of this day coming as a "*thief in the night*" emphasizes the surprise and unawareness each will have. God doesn't want your eyes physically peering off into the distance, paralyzed by your longing. Instead, He demands your hands be placed on the plow with eyes on the row ahead of you and planting the seed of the Word of God in those you meet daily. He wants you and I to be busy watering and caring for the growth of those developing a faith in the Lord.

Instead of a paralyzed gaze, Peter calls these Christians to live in a way that demonstrates a strong conviction and a bold proclamation that Jesus will return. This will impact everything from our attendance and participation in worship to our relationships within our marriages and with our children. The people with whom we work, see at the gym, or even go hunting should be able to see our expectations regarding the day of the Lord. In short, when we live with a *"looking"* and *"hastening"* for the coming of the day of God, there will be a significant, noticeable difference in our lives.

3) Be Diligent to be Found in Peace, Spotless, and Blameless

In 2 Peter, diligent or diligence is used multiple times.

- 1:5—*"Now for this very reason also, applying all **diligence**, in your faith supply moral excellence, and in your moral excellence, knowledge."*

- 1:10—*"Therefore, brethren, be all the more **diligent** to make certain about His calling and choosing you; for as long as you practice these things, you will never stumble."*

- 1:15—*"And I will also be **diligent** that at any time after my departure you will be able to call these things to mind."*

- 3:14—*"Therefore, beloved, since you look for these things, be **diligent** to be found by Him in peace, spotless and blameless."*

In each occasion, the emphasis behind the word involves being "especially conscientious in discharging an obligation, be zealous/eager, take pains, make every effort, be conscientious."[8] With conscientious effort being such a pivotal component, it should hit home that the determination required to be right before God will not happen by chance. That doesn't mean I'm advocating for any theory or teaching that claims to be able to earn our way into the category of "right" before God. However, I want to impress upon each of you that your relationship with God can't coast or exist passively and be pleasing to Him. You must pursue Him and pursue a life that aligns with what He expects, which aligns with His character. That's why in 2 Peter 1:5-7, Peter emphasizes that we must be determined to devote ourselves to continual growth in the spiritual virtues God sets forth.

In chapter 3, Peter specifically mentions three essential character traits that must be our pursuit. He does so while emphasizing the earnest effort and intention necessary. He admonishes the Christians to be determined to be found on the day of visitation…

1) In Peace (εἰρήνη, *eirēnē*)

When the day of the Lord is upon us, Jesus appears with His mighty angels in flaming fire, "*dealing out retribution to those who do not know God and to those who do not obey the gospel of our Lord Jesus*" (2 Thess. 1:8), the only thing that will matter is whether you are at war with God or not. It might sound strange to look at one's relationship with God in these terms; however, that's precisely what the Scriptures say regarding our condition when unforgiven sin stains our souls (Rom. 5:8-10).

As enemies of God, we desperately need forgiveness and justification that only God extends through the Gospel (Eph. 6:15). If we neglect such salvation, the abundance of tears poured forth on Judgment Day won't have the power to change our eternal state. However, if we embrace salvation in this life, as the Christians whom Peter is writing have (2 Pet. 1:1), peace ("a state of concord, harmony"[9]) will be ours. This is not a peace that results from an inner acceptance of ourselves or our circumstances. It's not peace that results from all the personal relationships in our lives being in harmony. Instead, the peace described here explicitly refers to the relationship between God and the individual sinner. This peace is only possible because God offers it and delivers it to the One who is the Prince of Peace, Jesus Christ (Isa. 9:6).

2) Spotless (ἄσπιλος, *áspilos*)

As a stark contrast to the false prophets described by Peter as "stains and blemishes" (2 Pet. 2:13), he further elaborates on the condition in which they are to be found upon the day of the Lord's appearance. Like a dirty garment needing to be cleansed by water and soap, we—because of our sins—have the same problem the children of God had in the day of the prophet Jeremiah when we wrote, *"'Although you wash yourself with lye and use much soap, the **stain** of your iniquity is before Me,' declares the Lord God"* (Jer. 2:22, emp. added). This condition puts us at odds with God and in alignment with those who live in rebellion.

As a comparison, in 1 Peter 1 Peter uses the word *"spotless"* to describe the nature of Jesus regarding His perfection and sacrifice when he wrote,

> *If you address as Father the One who impartially judges according to each one's work, conduct yourselves in fear during the time of your stay on earth; knowing that you were not redeemed with perishable things like silver or gold from your futile way of life inherited from your forefathers, but with precious blood, as of a lamb unblemished and **spotless**, the blood of Christ.* (1 Pet. 1:17-19, emp. added)

In this usage, we see the emphatic point being made that those who chose to live according to sensuality and greed, as the false prophets of 2 Peter, will find themselves outside of purification on the day recompense is heaped upon them. Regardless of how pleasing their words may be and how enticing their promises may seem, their conduct demonstrates that they live outside of the character and nature of Jesus Christ. Thus, they are as opposite as they can be to what God has shown He desires from His followers through the life of Jesus Christ.

3) Blameless (ἀμώμητος, *amōmētos*)

If you've ever built anything, you know blemishes exist. You know where the measurements were a 1/16th of an inch off or where the glue was pressed out between the joints and dried. If a board was twisted a little or had a bow in it and you had to make last-minute adjustments, that might not have been the best, but they worked. Any of us who have made anything knows this reality. Blemishes just seem to be a part of crafting something.

The blemishes sometimes add character or make one handcrafted piece unique and special. You realize this immediately when you walk through an antique store. Taking a quick trip through history, when many tools and pieces of furniture were handmade, reveals that imperfections will naturally be a part of the product when human hands are involved.

While that may be true when crafting items, it's also true when it comes to matters of a spiritual nature. Romans 3:23 makes it very clear that *"all have sinned and fall short of the glory of God,"* which indicates that spiritual blemishes will happen when it's left up to us as people. If that weren't true, we would not need Jesus. If we could live without spiritual blemishes, repentance, forgiveness, and redemption would be topics we wouldn't need to study and take personally. However, that's not the case. We need to hear and learn about these crucial topics because we can't save ourselves from our sins.

When Peter instructs the Christians to be found *"blameless,"* he's telling them to be people who are "without fault and therefore morally blameless."[10] In light of this charge, a tremendous and seemingly impassable mountain seems to be before us. Many of those who read this will think to themselves, "I can never be blameless!" Of your own accord, you absolutely can't. That's why we need the blood of Jesus to cleanse us. However, that doesn't mean we can't set our aim to live morally pure lives. That's the charge we see in Leviticus 18–20. The Israelites are called to live differently than those in the land of Canaan. We see the same thing in Peter's first letter to these Christians in 1 Peter 1:14-15. Even with you set your aim to live a morally pure life, you will fail. The great news is that it was never about your getting it all right anyway. It's always been about God making you blameless, without blemish, through the Gospel of Jesus Christ.

4) Be on Guard

Imagine your family being in an extremely crowded environment, much like you've seen in New York City on New Year's Eve. Everywhere you turn, with each move, you bump into someone. You can barely move, and when you can, you want your family to move as a unit because you know of the dangers that persist if you're separated or worse, there's a "bad guy" who is looking for ways to grab children in such an environment and disappear with them.

If you're like me, you are on heightened alert. You're constantly looking around and seeing if dangers exist or trying to find ways to maneuver your family through the crowd in the best way possible. You're also insistent on your family holding hands or grabbing onto one another's shirt/jacket and holding on. You need each family member to keep eyes on one another because the task is too great for one person to see everything and make the decisions necessary to navigate such a task.

If you've ever been in such an environment or can vividly imagine a situation as you read this, your blood pressure is probably increasing just a bit. You may even feel slightly uncomfortable as your nerves strike you more. Your breathing rate may have even increased as you began imagining some of the "what ifs" that a vivid illustration stirs. In this case, that's a good thing because I want you to relate to what it means to be on guard as Peter instructed the Christians in 2 Peter 3:17, "*You therefore, beloved, knowing this beforehand,* **be on your guard** *so that you are not carried away by the error of unprincipled men and fall from your own steadfastness*" (emp. added).

A heightened sense, keen awareness, a greater attention to detail, a determination to keep something or someone from being taken from you or from you losing it yourself, all these descriptions and human responses are wrapped into being on guard. While many of us are completely capable of associating these to our response to a crowded environment and our family, do we also understand the relation of this to our faith? Do we know the potential dangers that linger around the corners regarding our faith?

After identifying the false prophets—their teaching, techniques, and motivations—Peter calls to arms the determination and alertness of these Christians. He doesn't want them to fall away into the same mire; however, Peter understands, and he wants them to accept that if they are going to remain faithful in the face of such falsity, they must, just like we must, be alert, be aware, and be adamant about avoiding such threatening teaching and be grounded in the truth of God's Word as delivered by men inspired by the Holy Spirit (2 Pet. 1:20-21).

5) Grow in Grace and Knowledge

The best way to combat false teaching that seeks to ensnare us is to continually grow in the grace and knowledge of our Lord and Savior, Jesus Christ. Stagnation opens the door to considering all sorts of theories and beliefs, not having the drive nor the working knowledge that is sharp and keen to combat such. That's why Biblical illiteracy is such a dangerous condition. It's not only that one's faith grows stale. It's that the immaturity and lack of pursuit of a closer relationship with Jesus leaves us vulnerable to the attacks of Satan.

Think about your physical health. Lousy health will eventually take hold if you're not actively pursuing good health. A person who continues exercising, getting the right amount of sleep, drinking the right amount of water, and avoiding abundant sugar and fatty foods will move toward better health. His heart will get stronger, blood sugar will be regulated, and cholesterol will be kept in check. However, the opposite is true of the person who sits around, doesn't exercise, and has a "eat whatever I want" diet. While not necessarily actively pursuing early health problems, that person has not actively pursued better health.

The same applies when it comes to our spiritual well-being. It's like riding a bicycle. If you're moving forward, you stay up on the bike. The second you stop, it's much more challenging to balance and you fall off. If we aren't actively pursuing better spiritual health, by default we will find spiritual decline. Peter is admonishing them, as he did in 2 Peter 1:5-8, to determine to be right by growing, continually pushing forward, in the grace, the divine favor extended to people by God through Jesus Christ (2 Pet. 1:2), and knowledge, the unfiltered true knowledge, of our Lord and Savior Jesus Christ.

CONCLUSION

There is a fixed chasm between the person who merely wants to "look right" and the one who wants to "be right." One is self-seeking, and the other is rooted in integrity. "Looking right" is interested in pleasing man, while "being right" is focused on consistency regardless of whether men are pleased.

The imagery of those spoken of in Matthew 6 rises to the top when I think of the vast difference between these two. The hypocrites do good; however, it's all a show. They give so others will honor them (Matt. 6:2). They pray and want to make sure others see them (Matt. 6:5). The hypocrites fast. Still, they do so to be noticed by men (Matt. 6:16). In all these examples, the emphasis is placed on the reward man gives versus the much better reward God wants to give them. The problem is there's no room for God's reward in their lives.

When you and I think about being determined to be right, we're talking about your inner man, who you are at the core. Your motivations are being targeted. Your reasons for doing what you do are being questioned. While this may be uncomfortable, the answers you give when dealing with both reveal whether you are about "looking right" or "being right." God is the only One you need to be concerned with pleasing. He alone sets the standard in the lives of those who want to be His people. There is no room for a divided spirit in the ranks of Jesus Christ, so we must have a convicted determination to be the people He desires.

REFLECTION

1. What is the underlying difference between a person more concerned about looking right than being right?

2. In what ways do holy conduct and godliness entail purpose, intent, determination, and sacrifice?

3. How are you preparing for Jesus' return?

4. What is the difference between looking at everyone suspiciously and being on guard, as taught in 2 Peter 3?

5. What is the biggest threat spiritual stagnation introduces in your life? How does stagnation occur? What are three ways you can move beyond spiritual stagnation?

NOTES

CHAPTER 5
DETERMINED TO STAND

"The difference between men is in energy, in the strong will, in the settled purpose and in the invincible determination."[1]

- Vince Lombardi -

Special Section: Synonyms of *determined*:

Tenacious—**persistent in maintaining, adhering to, or seeking something valued or desired.**[2]

Tenacity, often associated with perseverance, determination, and resilience, plays a crucial role in shaping an individual's success and ability to overcome challenges. A tenacious person exhibits unwavering persistence in the face of adversity, possesses a strong sense of purpose, and refuses to be deterred by obstacles.

At the core of being tenacious lies an unyielding determination to achieve one's goals, regardless of the difficulties encountered. This persistence is fueled by a deep passion and commitment toward a particular objective, driving the individual to push through setbacks. Self-discipline is also a critical characteristic of tenacious people, often setting clear and actionable plans to achieve their aspirations. They are willing to work hard, understanding that success rarely comes easy.

Furthermore, tenacity is closely intertwined with resilience, the ability to bounce back from failures and setbacks more robust than before. A tenacious person views challenges as stepping stones towards growth, using each setback as a valuable lesson to improve and refine their approach. This resilience enables them to stay focused on their goals, even when faced with adversity, criticism, or rejection.

A tenacious person also possesses a strong sense of grit, a combination of passion and perseverance over the long haul. Grit drives individuals to stay committed to their goals, even when the initial excitement fades, or progress seems slow. It is the ability to maintain momentum, day in and day out, working steadily towards the desired outcome. Success is not achieved overnight; tenacious people know it results from consistent effort and dedication.

With all these qualities of a tenacious person in mind, consider their value when it comes to our walk with God. When faced with challenges or obstacles, having tenacity allows individuals to persevere and remain steadfast in their faith. This resilience enables believers to weather difficult times, trusting in God's plan and continuing to seek His guidance and support. Furthermore, tenacity fosters a deep commitment and dedication to living out one's faith daily, even when circumstances may be discouraging.

HISTORICAL EXAMPLE

Born on June 20, 1925, in Kingston, Texas, Audie Murphy's upbringing was marked by poverty and hardship. Raised in a large family, he found himself thrust into the responsibilities of adulthood at a young age following his father's abandonment and his mother's death. Despite these challenges, Murphy's indomitable spirit and unyielding determination remained undeterred. When war engulfed the world in the 1940s, he saw an opportunity to escape the confines of his circumstances and make a difference.

Enlisting in the United States Army at the age of 17, Audie Murphy embarked on a journey defining his legacy. His unwavering determination became evident from the moment he set foot on the battlefield. Assigned to the 3rd Infantry Division, Murphy found himself in the thick of combat in North Africa, Sicily, Italy, and eventually, France.

Murphy's courage and determination were put to the ultimate test during the Allied invasion of Italy. He led his men with unwavering resolve in the face of withering enemy fire, earning a battlefield commission and a reputation for fearlessness. Despite being wounded multiple times, Murphy refused to yield, pressing forward with an iron will that inspired those around him.

However, his actions in France would etch his name in military history. On January 26, 1945, near the village of Holtzwihr, Audie Murphy's valor reached its zenith. Faced with overwhelming German opposition, his company commander ordered a retreat. But Murphy, refusing to abandon his comrades, single-handedly held off an entire company of German soldiers for over an hour, directing artillery fire with a field telephone and mounting a desperate defense.

With bullets flying and shells exploding around him, Audie Murphy's determination never wavered. Armed with little more than a rifle and a handful of grenades, he repelled wave after wave of enemy attacks, inflicting heavy casualties and buying precious time for his fellow soldiers to regroup. Despite sustaining severe injuries, including wounds to his leg, Murphy refused to surrender, fighting on until reinforcements arrived.

For his extraordinary bravery and unwavering determination in the face of overwhelming odds, Audie Murphy was awarded the Medal of Honor, the highest military decoration awarded by the United States government. He demonstrated unparalleled determination and bravery throughout his military career, earning numerous awards and decorations, including the Distinguished Service Cross, two Silver Stars, and three Purple Hearts. His exploits made him a symbol of American resilience and grit, inspiring countless soldiers to rise above adversity and face their challenges with courage and determination.[3,4]

Catherine Susan "Kitty" Genovese was born in Brooklyn, New York, on July 7, 1935, to Vincent and Rachel Genovese. Kitty was a standout student at Prospect Heights High School. She was the eldest of five siblings and was known for her wit and humor. After witnessing a murder, her family relocated to New Canaan, Connecticut, but Kitty remained in New York City.

In the early morning hours of March 13, 1964, around 2:30 a.m., Kitty Genovese was making her way home from work when she encountered Winston Moseley, armed with a knife. Fleeing toward her apartment building, she was caught by the assailant who stabbed her while she cried for help. Despite her severe injuries, Genovese managed to crawl to the rear of her apartment building, out of sight of potential witnesses. However, ten minutes later, Moseley returned and subjected her to further violence. Genovese would succumb to her injuries en route to the hospital.

The New York Times initially reported that 37 people watched and did not intervene, sparking public outrage. While there is evidence that The Times got the details wrong, there were two neighbors who were there and did not act. One of those was named Karl Ross.

Intoxicated that night, Ross heard noises and, after deliberating, cracked open his door to investigate. He saw Genovese lying on the ground, still alive and attempting to speak, and Moseley stabbing her. He shut the door and called a friend to ask what to do. The friend said not to get involved.

Ross eventually climbed out his window and went to a neighbor's apartment. He called the police after hearing Sophie Farrar, the neighbor who found Kitty, call for someone to do so. Ross' explanation, "I didn't want to get involved," became the pivotal claim of what would later become known as the Bystander Effect—where individuals are less likely to help in a group setting.⁵

Psychologists Latané and Darley's research shed light on this phenomenon, attributing it to diffusion of responsibility. Their studies found that the more people present when distress occurs, the less likely anyone is to act to intervene. Of course, this study was initiated by the thought that so many of Genovese's neighbors heard the attack and did not get involved, much like Ross claimed. While the initial facts regarding the number of witnesses are disputed, the studies that have surfaced since have shown there may be something to the Bystander Effect.

Psychologists who have studied this effect claim three psychological factors are thought to facilitate bystander apathy. They are the feeling of having less responsibility when more bystanders are present (*diffusion of responsibility*), the fear of unfavorable public judgment when helping (*evaluation apprehension*), and the belief that because no one else is helping, the situation is not an emergency (*pluralistic ignorance*).⁶ Unfortunately, because of fear and a lack of personal responsibility, many dangers go unchecked by onlookers, and many needs go unmet by those who can help. Groupthink influences actions, and the consequences of such can haunt those who stood by while people got hurt, remained hungry, or froze in a homeless condition.

When we take the lessons learned from the Kitty Genovese murder and couple them with the studies done to try and identify why people could act but do not, a picture is painted of human hesitation. When we apply this to the instruction given in the book of Jude 3, admonishing the Christians to "*contend earnestly for the faith,*" the amplification of the urgent charge to appropriately defend and confront those who threaten the goodness and simplicity of the Gospel of Jesus Christ can introspectively be felt by all. If these Christians were aware, alert, and attentive to the "*certain persons*" of verse 4, people who have already infiltrated their ranks as they pretend to be part of the family of God, Jude's instruction would not be necessary.

The problem is, just like Karl Ross in the Genovese case, too many

Christians see the problem and close their doors, not wanting to get involved. The dreadful thinking that someone else will deal with the false teachers who are described as *"ungodly persons who turn the grace of our God into licentiousness and deny our only Master and Lord, Jesus Christ"* (v. 4) paralyzes many otherwise dedicated followers of Jesus. Thoughts about what other people might say about them if they do stand for the truth cause tremendous angst and fear take over, convincing the Christian that at least in doing and saying nothing, they don't run the risk of doing or saying the wrong thing. While doubting the severity of the situation, many believe that if it were really that urgent to put a stop to the influence of those who are *"grumblers, finding fault, following after their own lusts"* who *"speak arrogantly, flattering people for the sake of gaining an advantage"* (v. 16), someone in a leadership position would do it. However, that's not what Jude calls these Christians to think or do.

Being determined to take a stand can be terrifying to many. Reading the above paragraph might make you very uncomfortable, realizing you have always thought those same things as you stayed silent. Let me put your mind at ease, *"contending earnestly for the faith"* does not mean you have to be "big and bad" in your Christianity. It's not about looking for a fight or living life confrontationally, always being suspicious of everyone who teaches or preaches God's Word. It requires you to study the Word of God so you can tell when something is advocated or taught that does not follow what God says (2 Tim. 2:14-19). When someone teaches error, with great humility and the intent to help a brother, you pull him aside and point him to a fuller, more complete understanding of God's Word just as Priscilla and Aquila did for Apollos (Acts 18:23-28). However, that's not all *"contending earnestly"* entails. It also means living a merciful lifestyle as one who has received mercy from God (Jude 21-23). Don't be quick to "write them off" as a lost cause. Be patient with them, as you want others to be with you.

Some are not interested in adhering to the Word of God. Like those in the book of Jude, they are *"ones who cause divisions, worldly-minded, devoid of the Spirit"* (v. 19). Unfortunately, those who will not cease spitting on God and His Word require a firm rebuke, one that will prayerfully cause them to repent as they reconsider their stance before God. However, even if they do not repent, there will be times when the doctrine of the Gospel of Jesus Christ must be defended from evil attacks, even at the expense of friendships, acquaintances, and possibly your reputation. Perhaps that's why Jude wrote to the Christians, appealing to them to *"contend earnestly for the faith."* They would already be doing it if it were easy, but it's not. It's costly but necessary.

The Gospel is still the greatest answer to man's most dire need: forgiveness from sin. It's here we read and learn of the mercy of God, revealed through His Son Jesus. Herein, a desperate man, sin-sick in his very soul, finds hope and direction out of the mire of lost condition. It's not a neutral act when people twist and distort the Word of God to their own ends. Instead, it's an attempt to defame God and His glorious name. You would stand up for your loved ones if someone tried to do that. How much more should you stand up for the God of the faith that has been *"once for all handed down to the saints"* (v. 3)?

DISCUSSION

1) Taking a Stand Involves Risks

Satan operates very well in the shadows of fear. Fear of the unknown, of the "what-ifs," and of the stories heard regarding what happened to other people is the disguise Satan uses to manipulate and stagnate disciples of Jesus Christ. He doesn't have to tempt you to commit a "big" overt sin. Although, that seems to be what feeds him. He only must convince you that the risks are not worth action. Satan wants you to allow the possibilities of difficulties to dissuade you from advancing the cause of Christ. He doesn't care if you and I claim to be disciples as long as we are stuck in fear and do nothing.

In the Old Testament, we read of dedicated men and women who refused to allow the risks to silence them. Daniel refused to stop praying to God even when the decree from Darius went forth, knowing that being cast into the den of lions was the risk for doing so (Dan. 6:4-

10). Esther, knowing that to come into the inner court of the king without being summoned could result in death, bravely stood for the people of God as she requested the king's and Haman's presence at a banquet she would host (Est. 5:11; 6:4). Shadrach, Meshach, and Abednego risked being thrown into the furnace of blazing fire as they refused to bow when the music played (Dan. 3:8-18). Moses risked his own life when returning to Pharaoh, demanding the release of the large slave force of the Egyptians. As a result, the labor and toil of the Israelites increased, and Moses received criticism and isolation from those hurting even more (Ex. 5). David faced the giant, knowing the risk of losing life and freedom for his people (1 Sam. 17). Noah risked ridicule from those around him as he showed tremendous trust in God and His word regarding the pending flood (Heb. 11:7).

The New Testament is also filled with examples of the disciples of Jesus boldly standing in the face of immense risks. In Acts 7, we read of the death of a man named Stephen, a disciple of Jesus Christ and one known as having *"good reputation, full of the Spirit and of wisdom"* (Acts 6:3). He was a man described as being *"full of faith and of the Holy Spirit"* (Acts 6:5), "grace and power" (Acts 6:8), and one who was not hiding, "performing great wonders and signs among the people" (Acts 6:8). Even in the face of the angry mob who would eventually murder him, he continued proclaiming the goodness of God through Jesus. Peter and John refused to stop spreading the good news of Jesus Christ, risking imprisonment and further punishment (Acts 4:18-21). Paul embraced the excruciating risks to stand up for Jesus and advance His cause (2 Cor. 6:3-10). John realized the danger of standing for Jesus as he was exiled to the island of Patmos (Rev. 1:9). Then there are the martyrs of Revelation 6:9-11, those who *"had been slain because of the Word of God, and because of the testimony which they had maintained."*

How can one read these and not be moved in motivation?

The cold truth is there are always risks involved when you are determined to stand for something, regardless of what it is. Standing requires conviction, commitment, and an unwavering dedication to a cause or a side. Anytime you are that determined, others who do not see it the way you do and disagree with your conclusions will be unsettled at least and vengeful at worst. Those so determined to take a stand will face embarrassment as they are isolated, slandered, gossiped about, and publicly or privately ridiculed. Those who have come before us have faced years of imprisonment and even death for standing for Jesus Christ and the Word of God. Their examples serve as focusing reminders that to suffer for the sake of advancing the Kingdom of God is honorable and desirable and places you in a more intimate relationship with Jesus, as He is the most outstanding example of facing deadly risks for the sake of the worthy cause of salvation (1 Pet. 2:21-24).

2) Taking a Stand Involves Rewards

What thought comes to mind when reading Hebrews 11 and the names listed therein? Perhaps, for you, it's the bravery each displayed as their belief in God was coupled with faithful action, thus defining what true Biblical faith is. Others may think of the difficulty each faced and ponder whether they would have been able to do the same. I stop in my tracks and am humbled when I read, *"They were stoned, they were sawn in two, they were tempted, they were put to death with the sword; they went about in sheepskins, in goatskins, being destitute, afflicted, ill-treated (men of whom the world was not worthy), wandering in deserts and mountains and caves and holes in the ground"* (Heb. 11:37-38). I am challenged because I internally ask myself if I would do the same and what my breaking point would be. I am drawn into introspection as I consider the risks involved and the cost paid. Then I'm brought back to the grounding principle on which they all acted, as pointed out in Hebrews 11:16, *"But as it is, they desire a better country, that is, a heavenly one."*

The rewards of standing for the Lord and the faith *"which was once for all handed down to the saints"* (Jude 3) far surpass any consequences that may present themselves due to the risks involved. This truth is amplified when we reflect on the brevity of our lives on this present earth. When put into the proper perspective as James 4:14 does, and we accept the temporariness of our situation, we are also, just like David, drawn to begging God to make us know our end, the extent of our days, and just how transient we are on this present earth. As David reflected, so do we, *"Behold, You have made my days as handbreadths, and my lifetime as nothing in Your sight. Surely every man at his best is a mere breath"* (Ps. 39:5). As we personalize the brief nature of our time in this flesh, and we consider sacrificing whatever is required in the short term for eternity of reward, the "trade-off" is incomparable (Rom. 8:18).

What are these rewards?

For starters, in looking at Jude, we see that those who are determined to stand and *"contend earnestly for the faith"* (Jude 3) are in the category of people who have *"mercy," "peace,"* and *"love"* multiplied to them. *"Mercy"* spoken of here is from God and is the "kindness or concern expressed for someone in need."[7] *"Peace"* is also rooted in God and means "a state of well-being."[8] *"Love"* is the word *agápē* and means "the quality of warm regard for and interest in another."[9] All of these are multiplied or increased for those who are *"called," "beloved,"* and *"kept for Jesus Christ"* (Jude 1).

Other rewards addressed explicitly in the book of Jude are found at the end of the letter. In verse 21, we read, *"the mercy of our Lord Jesus Christ to eternal life."* This sweet, promised reward resulted from God forgiving our sins through His Son Jesus. The hope we have in His return is to anchor and compel us to continue *"building"* ourselves up in the faith, *"praying"* in the Holy Spirit, and *"waiting anxiously"* with great expectations (Jude 20-21). Expanding further on the rewards, Jude tells these Christians that in so standing for the Lord and *"contending for the faith,"* God is able to *"keep you from stumbling, and to make you stand in the presence of His glory blameless with great joy"* (v. 24). Because of the forgiveness He extends to those who endure the risks involved with following Him, having fully and continually submitted to the very Gospel they preach to others, God promises to the determined to endure, tremendous and sure rewards.

3) Taking a Stand Involves Resolve

It has been said, "If you want to make everybody happy, don't be a leader. Sell ice cream." While there is debate as to credit former Apple founder Steve Jobs or former University of Alabama head coach Nick Saban with this quote, the truth of the statement is not impacted. When you stick your neck out for a person, a purpose, or a pursuit, there will be those who stand ready to chop it off. Criticism is in no short supply for those who stand up and be leaders.

There will always be challengers who are contentious and contrary. Knocking someone down who dares to be different and go against the cultural norm seems to be a reality we live with daily. That's why so many Christians either stay seated or, worse, bow down to the idols presented by those who distort and blaspheme the excellent name and nature of God. They would rather be liked by making people happy, than standing and leading. However, that's not you. That's not the drive and motivation of those determined to be pleasing to God.

Standing requires a deep-rooted resolve that is unwavering and unbending. It begins with an unapologetic conviction that what you are standing for is truth; it matters and is desperately needed by the world around you. In our case, for the consideration of this book, Jude makes it very clear that *"the faith"* is valuable and worth *"contending earnestly"* for, meaning it's worth the intense effort required to do so. It is not forfeited to anyone, especially the *"certain persons"* of Jude 4. Therefore, this task takes great resolve, a "fixity of purpose.[10]" But a resolve to do what? Where are we to focus our resolve? Consider the following three areas.

A. Resolve to Teach the Faith

Biblical illiteracy is a significant problem in many homes and individual lives. Far too many people who profess to be followers of Jesus have dusty Bibles, lacking the natural oils from their fingers marking the well-worn pages. Even in our day, where Bibles are readily available through technology, some even being read to you, we still find a way to remain lacking. This doesn't mean that everyone who is a disciple of Jesus Christ is this way; however, in my time in ministry with adults and teens alike, I have found that knowledge of the Word of God is very surface as we are well positioned to know what the preacher says in his sermon, but not necessarily what God says in His Word. We can point fingers as to why this is the case; however, at the end of the day, the result of a lack of knowledge will be the same for us as it was for the children of God during the days of Hosea when the prophet wrote regarding God's reflection on His people,

> *My people are destroyed for lack of knowledge.*
> *Because you have rejected knowledge,*
> *I also will reject you from being My priest.*
> *Since you have forgotten the law of your God,*
> *I also will forget your children.* (Hos. 4:6)

Let it never be repeated that *"there arose a generation after them who did not know the Lord"* (Judg. 2:10). If there ever is, each preceding generation—no matter what level of faithfulness they claimed—failed to pass along the faith.

There are no bystanders in this task. It is not someone else's responsibility. It's yours, and it's mine. Every disciple of Jesus Christ must learn from the church in Thessalonica. We must be like those from whom *"the word of the Lord has sounded forth"* (1 Thess. 1:8). Like Timothy's grandmother Lois and his mother Eunice, we must teach the faith to our families (2 Tim. 1:5). With the aim of glorifying God and leading others to a close walk with Him, we must strive to be the faithful men of 2 Timothy 2:2 who teach others. We must begin with the elementary principles of the Scriptures; however, we must move to the more mature teachings of the Word (Heb. 6:1).

With a resolve to teach the faith, not only will we be forced to study more deeply the Word ourselves, but we will also help ensure our loved ones, our neighbors, and our fellow Christians aren't swept away by false teachers who twist and distort the Scriptures to their end. If they dreadfully do turn their backs, it won't be because they didn't know the truth. Sadly, it will be because they selfishly pursued their desires or even the comforts of personal relationships.

We must go out of our way, whatever the cost may be to us or our resources, to teach the faith because, as we read in 2 Timothy 3:16, *"All Scripture is inspired by God and profitable for teaching, for reproof, for correction, for training in righteousness: so that the man of God may be adequate, equipped for every good work."* As Jesus did in John 8, we must understand and teach others that freedom is not found in man's conclusions but rather in continuing in the Word (vv. 31-32).

B. Resolve to Live the Faith

Perhaps one of the biggest draws of Christianity for those who are immature or not Christians at all is the unmerited kindness disciples of Jesus show every day. From stocking food pantries, serving the homeless, clothing the needy, caring for widows in nursing homes, visiting the orphans in children's homes, collecting furniture for people who've lost everything in house fires, knitting blankets for cancer patients, sewing teddy bears for those in the children's hospital, working on a neighbor's car, building a handicap ramp at the home of someone in a wheelchair, going grocery shopping for an elderly neighbor, babysitting for a young married couple who never gets to go out on a date, and countless other service-oriented exercises, Christians have a remarkable impact on those who do not know Jesus by showing Him to them in the way they live and serve. Jesus did say it best when He said,

> *You are the salt of the earth; but if the salt has become tasteless, how can it be made salty again? It is no longer good for anything, except to be thrown out and trampled under foot by men. You are the light of the world. A city set on a hill cannot be hidden; nor does anyone light a lamp and put it under a basket, but on the lampstand, and it gives light to all who are in the house. Let your light shine before men in such a way that they may see your good works, and glorify your Father who is in heaven.* (Matt. 5:13-16)

This kindness, or "*mercy*," as Jude puts it in verses 22-23, is not only to be shown to those who look favorably on Jesus and the Word of God. Regardless of their current view of Christianity, the disciple of Jesus is resolved to live the faith before all because he knows a day of judgment is coming. He wants even those who twist and distort the Word of God for their dishonest gain to glorify God on the day of visitation. As Peter wrote concerning those who would wish to cause Christians harm, we must keep our "*behavior excellent among the Gentiles, so that in the thing in which they slander you as evildoers, they may because of your good deed, as they observe them, glorify God in the day of visitation*" (1 Pet. 2:12).

That's because, as a Christian, your life is all about bringing honor and glory to God, both in your short stay on this earth and in eternity. You've died to yourself and are determined to stay behind the cross of Christ (Gal. 2:20). You want others to do the same, not residing on the receiving end of the wrath of God when Jesus returns (2 Thess. 1:7-8). Therefore, you must be resolved to show them the faith is not lip service meant to make you appear suitable but is a life-changing message that infiltrates your entire being. It's transforming your mind, energizing your actions, and softening your heart to those who desperately need us who have received mercy from God through Jesus to pour forth mercy on others around them.

C. Resolve to Defend the Faith

What does it mean to defend anything? What comes to mind when you consider a football game and the term "goal line" defense? My mind thinks of the severity of the situation. Defenses are only needed when something is worth defending, and the goal line qualifies because points are awarded if the offense crosses the line. The game could be won or lost on the ability of the defense to hold the line, not giving any ground to the opposing side.

In the special historical study at the beginning of this chapter, you read of Audie Murphy, a decorated World War

II hero who exemplified the significance of defending with unwavering resolve. On January 26, 1945, near the village of Holtzwihr, Murphy's valor shone brightly amidst the chaos of battle. Surrounded by advancing German forces, Murphy's small unit faced overwhelming odds. Despite the dangerous situation, Murphy refused to yield an inch of ground, embodying the indomitable spirit of defense. Just as Murphy stood firm against the tide of tyranny, we too must stand resolute in the face of those who would seek the destruction of the faith.

Please do not misunderstand. Quarrels and debates are not the goal. When they become the goal, the focus turns to winning an argument and not necessarily on winning the person or the people who listen for the cause of Christ. That doesn't mean I think conversations, call them "debates" if you'd like, that we see some having today are valueless. I do believe they have their place; however, at any time we turn an opportunity to discuss or debate the faith with others, and it turns into something that is about us, we are wrong.

We must resolve to defend the faith because of where it's seated and what is accomplished in the life of the person who obediently conforms to its teaching. God is the author of the faith, and Jesus is the good news of the faith. The grace and mercy of God have been extended to mankind in the simple fact that we have the faith that was delivered once for all handed down to the saints. God desires a relationship with each of us, that includes those who may not care right now. That perfect love is worth defending because it is rooted in the One who is perfect.

Through the faith, those who will submit and obey will find hope, peace, mercy, grace, and forgiveness. They will find the answer for better well-being, marriages, parenting, and societies. In the faith, we find a community of believers called the Church, a community that is family, bears the burdens of one another, and supports each other. We find purpose, meaning, and ultimately, what love truly is as we discover what God has done for us in sending His Son to die on the cross for our sins (John 3:16).

It's not about simply winning an argument. It's about being so grateful for what God has done for you that you want to honor Him. Like David was furious and taken back (1 Sam. 17) when he found the armies of Saul sitting back, allowing pagan Goliath to insult the very God whose banner they marched under, you and I must resolve to respond. David didn't understand how anyone who truly has faith in God could allow an attack on God, and neither should we. Fear and uncomfortableness are often realities of standing up and defending the faith. We must put those behind us because the cause is too valuable. Hold the line. Hold the post—not for your benefit, but so that the faith is not defamed—and others will want the blessings found therein.

CONCLUSION

The Bystander Effect is real. I'll never forget watching a video report of an older man who was robbed by an individual in a convenience store parking lot. The assailant was a much younger and stronger man who was bound and determined to take whatever he could from this older man. At one point in the video, the older man was standing in the gap between the car and the open driver's side door when the young man began slamming the door on the older man's legs. If he couldn't get the man's money or car, the criminal was going to make sure the older man paid with pain and possibly his life.

The news report wasn't about how horrible crime has become in some parts of America, although that definitely could have been its focus. Instead, during the report, the camera panned out, showing a crowd of witnesses who were stood by and did nothing while the older man was fighting for his life. The segment was a wake-up call that highlighted the condition of many in our culture who are too complacent in the face of danger.

We've become that way religiously as well. In our time, to be labeled intolerant, judgmental, or any number of negative terms terrifies far too many. The fear of what could happen if we got involved causes many to keep walking by as if they saw and heard nothing. What a shame!

Instead, we need to be people determined to stand for the faith. Yes, society is growing ever more secular, and the watered-down interpretations of the Word of God are popular. That's exactly what Paul told Timothy would happen (2 Tim. 4:1-4). The good news is that people are watching and wanting to see authenticity in many different facets of society. They want to see how the faith makes a difference in your life. They need to see if what you say, you believe—really believe. Will you live it out? Will those who've received mercy show mercy? Will those who preach the love of God display that when it comes to interactions, even with those who disagree with them? In short, they may not be as closed to God as they've been painted to be. Instead, they may be closed to those who profess to be His disciples who don't believe the faith is worth standing for.

Be determined to stand. The rewards outweigh the risks, and with great resolve, we can show our families, communities, country, and world that Jesus makes all the difference. Be determined!

REFLECTION

1. When considering the case of Kitty Genovese's murder, how did "groupthink" influence the actions of those who heard her and observed the situation? When it comes to Christianity, how does "groupthink" come into play? How does this influence the actions of people today?

2. Why do you think taking a stand for the faith terrifies many? What are some of the factors a person often processes and considers when the moment to take a stand occurs?

3. Briefly discuss the risks involved in taking a stand for the faith and the rewards for such. How do you determine whether or not the rewards outweigh the risks?

4. What is "resolve," and why is this crucial to taking a stand? How can a person develop such if they don't have the resolve to stand?

NOTES

DETERMINED ENDNOTES

CHAPTER 1

1. "Jesse Owens Quotes." BrainyQuote.com. BrainyMedia Inc, 2024. 10 January 2024. https://www.brainyquote.com/quotes/jesse_owens_166163.

2. Matthew Josephson and Robert E Conot, "Thomas Edison." Encyclopedia Britannica, 25 Dec. 2023, https://www.britannica.com/biography/Thomas-Edison.

3. https://www.goodreads.com/author/quotes/3091287.Thomas_A_Edison.

4. William Arndt et al., *A Greek-English Lexicon of the New Testament and Other Early Christian Literature* (Chicago: University of Chicago Press, 2000), 243.

5. Gurnek Bains, "Why Do Resolutions So Often Fail? | Psychology Today" *Psychology Today*, 31 Dec. 2021, www.psychologytoday.com/us/blog/global-lens/202112/why-do-resolutions-so-often-fail.

6. Arndt et al. 774.

7. Arndt et al. 939.

8. Arndt et al. 387.

9. Arndt et al. 316.

10. Arndt et al. 1029.

11. Arndt et al. 824.

12. Arndt et al. 824.

13. Mike Figliuolo, "The Difference Between Talkers and Doers" thoughtLEADERS, LLC: Leadership Training for the Real World. https://www.thoughtleadersllc.com/wp-content/uploads/2022/04/logo.png, 8 July 2020, www.thoughtleadersllc.com/2012/11/the-difference-between-talkers-and-doers/.

CHAPTER 2

1. https://www.azquotes.com/quotes/topics/determination.html.
2. "Purposeful." *Merriam-Webster.com Dictionary*, https://www.merriam webster.com/dictionary/purposeful.
3. William Arndt et al., *A Greek-English Lexicon of the New Testament and Other Early Christian Literature* (Chicago: University of Chicago Press, 2000), 945.
4. Arndt et al., 880.
5. Dr. Terry Mortenson, "Six Literal Days." *Answers in Genesis* (Answers In Genesis, 8 Feb. 2017), https:answersingenesis.org/days-of-creation/six-literal-days/.
6. John C. Maxwell, *The 21 Irrefutable Laws of Leadership* (Nashville: Thomas Nelson, 1998), 71.
7. World History Edu. "The Ancient City of Jericho: History and Major Facts." *World History Edu*, 10 Oct. 2023, worldhistoryedu.com/the-ancient-city-of-jericho-history-and-major-facts/.
8. Nathan Steinmeyer, "What Are the Dead Sea Scrolls?" *Biblical Archaeology Society*, 17 Apr. 2023, www.biblicalarchaeology.org/daily/biblical-artifacts/dead-sea-scrolls/what_are_the_dead_sea_scrolls/.
9. F. F. Bruce, "Josephus, Flavius," ed. D. R. W. Wood et al., *New Bible Dictionary* (Leicester, England; Downers Grove: InterVarsity Press, 1996), 611.
10. Derek Brown, "Tacitus," ed. John D. Barry et al., *The Lexham Bible Dictionary* (Bellingham: Lexham Press, 2016).

CHAPTER 3

1. https://www.overallmotivation.com/quotes/determination-quotes/.
2. "Intent," Merriam-Webster, https://www.merriam-webster.com/dictionary/intent.
3. Carol W Gelderman, "Henry Ford," *Encyclopedia Britannica*, https://www.britannica.com/biography/Henry-Ford.
4. Nathan Steinmeyer, History.com Editors, "Henry Ford," *History.com*, A&E Television Networks, 26 Mar. 2020, www.history.com/topics/inventions/henry-ford.
5. William Arndt et al., *A Greek-English Lexicon of the New Testament and Other Early Christian Literature* (Chicago: University of ChicagoPress, 2000), 520.
6. Arndt et al., 821.
7. Arndt et al., 1018.
8. Arndt et al., 5.

CHAPTER 4

1. "Determination Quotes: A-Z Quotes," *A*, www.azquotes.com/quotes/topics/determination.html?p=7.
2. "Adamant," Merriam-Webster, https://www.merriam-webster.com/thesaurus/adamant.
3. Bosley Crowther, "Walt Disney," *Encyclopedia Britannica*, 19 Jan. 2024, https://www.britannica.com/biography/Walt-Disney.
4. Arndt et al., 11.
5. Arndt et al., 412.
6. Arndt et al., 877.
7. Arndt et al., 938.
8. Arndt et al., 939.
9. Arndt et al., 287.
10. Arndt et al., 56.

CHAPTER 5

1. Vince Lombardi Quotes," BrainyQuote.com. BrainyMedia Inc, 2024, 10 February 2024, https://www.brainyquote.com/quotes/vince_lombardi_786504.
2. "Tenacious," *Merriam-Webster*, https://www.merriam-webster.com/dictionary/tenacious.
3. Evan Andrews, "WWII Hero Audie Murphy: 'How Come I'm Not Dead?'" *History.Com*, 23 Jan. 2015, www.history.com/news/audie-murphys- world-war-ii-heroics-70-years-ago.
4. Richard L Rodgers, "Biography," *Audie Murphy Research Foundation*, 1996, www.audiemurphy.com/biography.htm.
5. Editors, History.com, "Kitty Genovese—Case, Murder, and Bystander," History.Com, 5 Jan. 2018, www.history.com/topics/crime/kitty-genovese.
6. Ruud Hortensius and Beatrice de Gelder, "From Empathy to Apathy: The Bystander Effect Revisited," *Current Directions in Psychological Science* Vol. 27,4 (2018): 249-256.
7. William Arndt et al., *A Greek-English Lexicon of the New Testament and Other Early Christian Literature* (Chicago: University of Chicago Press, 2000), 316.
8. Arndt et al., 287.
9. Arndt et al., 6.
10. "Resolve," *Merriam-Webster*, https://www.merriam-webster.com/dictionary/resolve.

www.ingramcontent.com/pod-product-compliance
Lightning Source LLC
Chambersburg PA
CBHW061802070526
44586CB00023B/2681